BUILDING BRIDGES,
CROSSING BORDERS

❋

BUILDING BRIDGES, CROSSING BORDERS

One Young Deaf Woman's Education

Ann Darby Getty

Gallaudet University Press
Washington, DC

Gallaudet University Press
Washington, DC 20002
http://gupress.gallaudet.edu

Library of Congress Cataloging-in-Publication Data

Getty, Ann Darby.
  Building bridges, crossing borders : one young deaf woman's education /
  Ann Darby Getty.
    pages cm
  ISBN 978-1-56368-607-8 (paperback) -- ISBN 978-1-56368-608-5 (e-book)
  1. Deaf--Education. I. Title.
  HV2430G354 2014
  371.91'2092--dc23
  [B]
                                                    2013046134

Contents

Foreword   vii

Acknowledgments   ix

Introduction   1

Chapter 1: Lessons from the Past   13

Chapter 2: Freedom to Thrive   26

Chapter 3: Field of Dreams   41

Chapter 4: Meet the Daniels Family   58

Chapter 5: School Choice   91

Chapter 6: College and Beyond   108

Chapter 7: Lessons Learned—A Cautionary Tale   124

References   139

Index   153

Foreword

I began this writing with the end goal of being able to complete a dissertation . . . and obtain a doctorate in the field of education. This doctorate, a framed piece of paper now hanging on my wall, was a lifelong dream, complicated by the requirement of a final piece of research. Research to me meant attempting to create meaning by applying a mathematical formula to a situation and coming up with findings previously undiscovered. Despite having had multiple courses in statistics and a wonderful professor, the mere thought of such an endeavor made me physically ill. I shall be eternally grateful for the person/s who came up with the notion of qualitative research, where one can use words rather than numbers to tell a story, make discoveries, and create new understandings . . . understandings considered to be significant (not statistically significant, of course) but significant in ways that contribute to living. Who would have thought that stories could lead to profound discovery and would in fact be considered by dissertation committees to be works of academic substance? I shall be forever thankful for that bit of grace.

Should the privilege of working on my doctorate have been afforded during my younger years, my dissertation story would no doubt have been very different. At that time, I thought I knew the formula for teaching children who are deaf. Doubtless I would have written with great authority and conviction. My perception of the story lived and shared by Kyler Daniels and her parents would have fit into a neat little preconceived framework, a blueprint to be read and followed . . . a blueprint filled with fallacies. Thankfully with age comes wisdom, and the ability to realize that real life cannot be prescribed, nor predetermined. It comes at us daily in fits and jerks, blinding us by the unexpected (just after we think we have it all figured out), reminding us that we are not in control.

My greatest desire is that readers will use this book in ways that will best suit their needs. If a family is in the throes of decision making after their child has been identified as having a severe to profound hearing loss, it may be more beneficial to read the introduction and then go straight to Chapter 4 without taking time to read Chapters 1 through 3. There may be a need to know the outcome without delay, and to be able to utilize that information as the decision-making process unfolds. However, I must advise that the story of a single individual and her family cannot be perceived to be a universal experience. It is one story among many, each with differing outcomes . . . some very positive and conversely, some less so. It would be prudent to then return to Chapters 1 through 3 in order to develop an awareness of the issues faced by d/Deaf peoples historically and the warring philosophies that continue to influence people within the field. It is only within a historical context of Deaf education, that an understanding of points of view and perspectives can be understood and appreciated.

As students entering the field of d/Deaf education, for those of us who are lifelong learners and those in fields surrounding Deaf education, this text is one that should make us ponder our philosophical certainties, convictions, and educational mantras as we seek to work with families of d/Deaf children who are desperately in need of our support. This support needs to be present regardless of the decisions parents make for their children.

Parents and professionals must come to the realization that there is no single, perfect educational situation or setting. There is rather, a rich tapestry of factors that contribute to student success, many of which will be explored as we move forward. Bottom line: where there is a loving and supportive family, and dedicated teachers, there is a mountain of hope.

Acknowledgments

My deep appreciation goes to Gallaudet University Press for this once in a lifetime opportunity. Specifically, I wish to thank Ivey Pittle Wallace and Deirdre Mullervy. Despite my initial concerns Ivey provided encouragement, enthusiasm, and deep insight into this project. Under Deirdre's watchful eye, words were transformed into cohesive thoughts. I would also like to thank Carol Hoke, who edited and reviewed my work. I am in awe of her talent. They have my deepest gratitude, admiration, and respect.

Thanks also goes to my professors and mentors at West Virginia University for suggesting that I write a book; their encouragement and confidence provided me with the impetus to attempt the otherwise unthinkable. Most especially, I would like to thank Dr. Elizabeth Dooley . . . how truly blessed I was to have been under her tutelage; her wisdom and unwavering support will forever be remembered. My deep appreciation goes to Dr. Jan Hafer, former colleague and true friend, who never gave up on the eventuality of this book.

Without the support, assistance, and guidance of others this work would never have come to fruition. I am thankful beyond words for the many opportunities I have been given in the field of Deaf education, for the gift of friendship and intellectual stimulation from my colleagues throughout the years as well as from the families whose children I have had the privilege to teach. I thank (the late) Dr. McCay Vernon, my first professor and mentor . . . it was his work that brought me into the field and his energy that ignited my passion.

The importance and need for family support can never be underestimated, and in that regard I have been truly blessed. First, I thank my parents, Dr. Darrel and Laura Darby, who were my first teachers and mentors. Their legacy is that of dreaming the impossible . . . then accomplishing it. They are an incredible act to follow. I thank my siblings, extended family members and friends on whose shoulders I have cried; their ability to listen and encourage will forever be appreciated.

My husband, Greg, has been lavish with his words of encouragement and support, never wavering in his effort to convince me that this endeavor was one that was indeed possible—most especially during those times when I thought it to be just beyond my grasp. For him . . . there simply are no words. I thank my daughters, Meghan and Morghan from whom I am always learning. I appreciate so much their support during this undertaking. I cannot imagine this world without their sparkling personalities.

Finally, I thank the Daniels family, Ginny, Bob, and Kyler. It has been an amazing twenty-three-year odyssey! They have opened their home and hearts, entrusted me with their deepest thoughts, endured hours of interviews, and have allowed me to share a small part of who they are in the following pages. Their friendship will be forever cherished.

Introduction

This book is the culmination of more than thirty-five years of experience in the field of Deaf education. It explores a variety of hot-button topics, discussions, and dilemmas currently faced by parents of deaf children and the professionals who serve them. These issues are confronted as each comes into play in the life of Kyler, a young deaf woman, who was born to hearing parents Bob and Ginny Daniels. Kyler was born in December of 1988 and was identified as having a profound, bilateral hearing loss at the age of 12 months. Her story unfolds from the time of her initial identification to the present, with Kyler's current status as a twenty-three-year-old college graduate, professional artist, and veterinary assistant.

Educational decisions and medical interventions are explored via numerous interviews, at times with mother and daughter together and at other times with Ginny and Kyler separately. Our discussions occurred over the course of 3 years and included times of laughter, joy, and tears as we reminisced about the good times and those that were not quite so good. Bob's participation in the discussion was less extensive than that of Ginny and Kyler, due to greater constraints on his work schedule and availability. However, his voice lends a very meaningful perspective: that of his journey to come to grips with his daughter's deafness. He describes the initial anger and darkness that devoured him and the transformation that occurred as he watched Kyler grow, learn, and flourish.

In addition, raw text such as educational records (including individualized educational programs pre-K through 12th grade), results of educational and audiological evaluations, as well as medical evaluations and follow-up reports from Kyler's cochlear implant surgery from its initiation to the present, are examined.

Kyler's artwork is highlighted, and the notion that sign language has positively affected her visual-spatial imagery and artistic talent is explored. Art is also examined as an integral device through which Kyler views her world and engages in self-expression.

The results of sifting through educational, medical, and personal documents and selecting that which most richly depicts the phenomenon embedded within the context of Kyler's experience have produced the experiential text that is our shared story. We gathered around my kitchen table sometimes with a plate of cookies or pizza within hands reach and always with our bottles of Smart Water hoping that it would be true to its name and help us recall with clarity experiences from our past. The tape recorder was situated in the middle recording the words that flowed forth as we pondered how it was that we had come to this place in our lives . . . Kyler reaching adulthood with a good self-image, Ginny arriving thus far with her sanity intact, Bob having shed his demons, and I having grown in ever so many ways as a result of our shared lives. Drinking our water, we chatted through the changing seasons, Ginny and Kyler interrupting one another as mothers and daughters do, at times interviewing one another with me becoming the listener. Kyler and I signed and spoke simultaneously during the sessions while Ginny spoke unaccompanied by signs. While simultaneous communication is no longer a requirement for Kyler, she and I resorted to communicating the way we always have, a carryover from the past. After our shared discussions, I would retreat to my computer and painstakingly type every word that had been spoken, which would more often than not lead to a new list of questions and topics to be queried.

There is, as well, an ongoing discursive text that runs throughout the book and situates this narrative within broader discourses such as issues among and concerns of professionals in the field of deaf education, dilemmas and decisions faced by hearing parents of deaf children, and the way in which Kyler, a cochlear implant recipient, has responded to a choice that was made in her stead.

Finally, circumstances that have led to Kyler's ability to cross borders or boundaries imposed by philosophies held in the field of Deaf education and those within her home community are identified, as well as factors that have allowed Kyler to define who she is and determine who she will become.

Much of the information contained in this text was first presented as a doctoral dissertation. As a result of encouragement from my dissertation committee, the willingness of Ginny, Bob, and Kyler Daniels to disclose their story, and the need for parents of newly identified d/Deaf children to be able to benefit from the experience of others, I share what we have learned as teacher, student, and parents. It is my sincere hope that information put forth in this text will encourage, inspire, and provide insight into all that is possible for deaf children born to hearing parents and will help identify struggles that may be faced and criticisms that may occur regardless of the path/s chosen. This is a book for parents, grandparents, and family members of newly identified deaf children. May it shed light on your journey and provide a wealth of information, knowledge, and resources to assist in making the best possible decisions for your child. Although the book has been written from the perspective of a deaf child of hearing parents, some of the decisions made and their implications may also resonate with Deaf parents of Deaf children.

This book is also written for evolving professionals in the field of Deaf education. So often we adopt a philosophy, draw a line in the sand, and assume our place on a soapbox without calling to mind that every "rule of thumb" has its exceptions and every philosophy its antithesis. My hope is that, as you encounter the readings contained in this text, as well as future readings of texts, documents, and research, you will weigh and measure each approach, idea, and philosophy in the context of what is best for the individual child, bearing in mind the uniqueness of each. Every child you teach comes to you with a story, with a parent or parents who have had to make mammoth decisions regarding what is best for their child, often while receiving competing or contradictory information from professionals who may on occasion share opinions in an overbearing or a biased manner. Regardless of one's own philosophy of education, we have yet as a profession to discover the Holy Grail or an elixir that works impartially on each and every student who enters the classroom. Keeping that thought in mind, we must always allow for the possibility that shifting paradigms and wisdom gained through experience may lead to a professional epiphany. As professionals, we must remain open to the lessons learned from the students and families whom we have the privilege to interact with and serve. Lyricist Oscar Hammerstein II, in *The King and I*, summarizes what should be the desired experience of all teachers: "if you become a teacher, by your pupils you'll be taught."

The title of the book, *Building Bridges, Crossing Borders*, comes from the notion that all parents and all teachers want their children or students to gain the tools needed to build bridges. Such bridge-building tools include the ability to communicate, to learn, and to make decisions—in short, to chart one's course. Bridges allow one to cross borders or boundaries . . . experience worlds not yet known, create, invent, discover, and initiate new beginnings. Bridges allow us to escape the boundaries imposed by others, mingle with those we may have considered "different," and learn in the process how very much we are alike.

Parents and professionals benefit tremendously from the study of deaf students who have successfully engaged in a learning process that has brought about positive results. Stories of those who have faced similar situations are valuable in that they give us an opportunity to learn from the experience of others, to isolate scenarios that lead to social and academic success, and to identify events or occurences that may create barriers to learning and to engage with society at large. This story follows a twenty-three-year span in the life of a young deaf woman, as it is situated in the history of d/Deaf peoples, and the ongoing philosophical debates pertaining to communication issues, the use of amplification (cochlear implants in particular), and educational options. Hopes, dreams, and concerns, both parental and personal, are shared during the course of informal conversations.

In the case of Kyler, her challenge as a young deaf person growing up in a rural community with few deaf and/or hard of hearing peers or d/Deaf adult role models is explored, as well as her response to being among the first cadre of deaf children to receive a cochlear implant at the age of 3, a practice that is now commonplace.

I made the acquaintance of Kyler and her mother as a result of a referral from a local pediatrician when Kyler was approximately 13 months of age. Kyler was born with congenital bilateral deafness due to unknown causes following an uncomplicated pregnancy and delivery. Due to the lack of neonatal hearing screening (which would have identified the hearing loss prior to hospital discharge) and Kyler's keen visual response to vibration and movement, her hearing loss was not medically determined until 12 months of age, when she was evaluated at the insistence of her mother.

Kyler and her family are Caucasian and are of middle-class socioeconomic status. They live in a rural, mountainous community in the mideastern region of the United States. Kyler's mother, Ginny, has a college degree and is employed by the state in which she resides as an activity therapy associate and a nursing assistant. Her father, Bob, is the foreman of a city property improvement program. Both parents have normal hearing, and there is no known history of deafness on either side of the family. With the exception of not being able to hear, Kyler was normal in all other respects having age-appropriate cognitive, motor, and psychosocial development. I began working with Kyler on a twice-weekly basis shortly after she was identified as being deaf and continued to do so for the following 2 years on a voluntary basis. I introduced sign language immediately, and Ginny continued to talk to Kyler, reinforcing her speech with signs as she added them to her repertoire.

In addition to learning sign language as it was introduced during home visits, Ginny, Bob, and other family members took sign language classes at a local community college. Newly acquired signs were introduced to Kyler during her daily interactions with family members. Kyler started signing quickly, following the normal language pattern of using a single sign/word (e.g., *eat, drink, car*) and within several months was beginning to put two to three signs together. She was fitted with binaural hearing aids following an audiological evaluation that resulted in gaining measurable hearing thresholds. Unfortunately, responses to the pure tones that occurred in the testing booth did not translate to usable hearing for Kyler. After many months, the hearing aids proved to be of no benefit in terms of accessing residual hearing. A vibrotactile aid was used to determine whether vibration might provide additional stimuli, but it too proved to be of little, if any, value.

In addition, Kyler was served by teachers from the state school for deaf children, who made home visits on a weekly basis. They introduced additional signs, modeled signing in the context of everyday situations, and provided a variety of learning opportunities through structured play. The philosophy these teachers followed was that of a bilingual/bicultural model in which American Sign Language is used rather than a signed English system. Amer- ican Sign Language (ASL) is not English; rather, it has its own distinct morphology and syntax (Hoemann, 1976, p. vii).

Kyler also received speech therapy services through the public school system. The initial focus during those sessions was primarily on vocal production as the therapist did not know sign language and had no previous experience working with a deaf population. However, therapy shifted to the development of auditory discrimination skills, English language usage, pragmatics, and self-monitoring when Kyler entered kindergarten and continued thereafter. At home, Kyler's mother continued to sign and speak simultaneously when communicating with or in front of Kyler.

Kyler entered the public school system as a preschool child (at the age of 4) and participated in a newly formed class for deaf and hard of hearing children. There were generally five to seven students in the multiage class, with ages differing by as many as 5 years. A certified teacher of deaf students and two instructional assistants supervised the self-contained classroom. This was the beginning of what would continue to be Kyler's primary instructional setting throughout her elementary school years with access to an 'inclusion' environment with normal hearing peers increasing as Kyler was able to benefit.

Instruction was provided in a Total-Communication framework, which incorporated the use of amplification, Signed English, and simultaneous spoken English. Signed English is an educational tool meant to be used while speaking, thereby helping one communicate with deaf children and normal hearing individuals who, for a variety of reasons, are experiencing difficulty in their development of spoken language (Bornstein, Saulnier, & Hamilton, 1983, p. 2).

In the meantime, as Kyler did not respond to auditory stimuli, her parents explored the option of a cochlear implant. A cochlear implant is very different from a hearing aid. Hearing aids simply amplify sound. Cochlear implants bypass the damaged portions of the ear and directly stimulate the auditory nerve. Signals generated by the implant are sent by way of the auditory nerve to the brain, which recognizes the signals as sound. Such hearing is quite different from normal hearing and requires time to learn to discriminate the meaning of the various pure-tone sounds. Implants do not result in normal hearing. Results vary in terms of the degree of benefit. An implant allows some people to do no more than recognize warning signals. However, others may enjoy full access to conversational speech, acquire intelligible speech, or be able to converse by telephone.

When Kyler reached school age, her parents chose to keep her in the local school system, during which time a satellite program was initiated. This program, which involved a collaborative effort between the county public school system and the state school for deaf students, continued through Kyler's graduation from elementary school. Thereafter, collaboration from the school for deaf students occurred only when input was sought by the county supervisor of special education or Kyler's classroom teachers.

Kyler's instruction throughout elementary school occurred in a self-contained classroom with other deaf and hard of hearing students. She was initially "included" with hearing children only for art and physical education classes with the assistance of an instructional assistant who signed. By the third grade Kyler was included for academic subjects such as science and social studies; however, all of the topics were reinforced, and background information was expanded in the self-contained classroom setting.

My role as an educator, while prominent during Kyler's preschool years, diminished entirely until grades 3 to 5 when I served as her interpreter for resource classes such as art, physical education, and media. During grades 4 and 5, science and social studies were added to classes in an integrated environment. At that time, I interpreted, previewed, and reviewed subject matter for those courses.

During Kyler's middle school years, I had no involvement in her academic instruction as I was teaching full-time at the elementary level. I resumed working with Kyler during grades 9 through 11, at which time I coordinated her interpreter and note-taking services and met with her daily for a study hall period to review and clarify coursework.

Suffice it to say, my role in Kyler's formal education waxed and waned and was dependent on her programming needs and my changing roles within the school system. A constant in our relationship throughout her years of public schooling was the interactions between our families, which occurred on a regular basis.

Kyler followed the same academic format throughout middle school, moving between the regular education classrooms, with instruction interpreted by the teacher of deaf students or an instructional assistant. She remained in the self-contained classroom for reading, language arts, and additional academic support.

By the time Kyler reached high school, the federally mandated No Child Left Behind legislation had come into play, at which time she was fully "included" in regular education merit classes with an interpreter and a note taker for all classes. She was provided with a study hall period, during which she received support for the first year from a certified teacher of deaf students and thereafter from a regular education teacher who had no signing skills. At that time, an interpreter was made available during the study hall sessions. Kyler received speech therapy five times a week while in elementary school and two to three times a week throughout middle school and high school, during which time she made good progress in both auditory discrimination abilities, language usage, and speech intelligibility. Amazingly enough, Kyler's speech therapist was the same person throughout her kindergarten and middle school years, an occurrence that no doubt was a positive factor in the development of Kyler's auditory discrimination abilities and spoken language.

During high school, Kyler continued to associate mainly with one other female deaf student and made only a few close hearing friends. She did well academically and was the recipient of a women's history award. Additionally, Kyler became the first deaf student in her county to be inducted into the National Honor Society. She also participated in athletics, playing on the freshman basketball team and running track during all four years of high school. By the time she graduated from high school, her speech was intelligible to those familiar with her speech pattern and to most new acquaintances, which allowed her to carry on extended verbal conversations in quiet settings.

Socially, Kyler attended school functions, dances, and extracurricular activities typical of her peers. Additionally, she won numerous awards for her artistic endeavors throughout elementary, middle, and high school.

Kyler graduated in the spring of 2012 from a local university, where she received a bachelor of fine arts degree in art and design with a minor in art history. Prior to that, she attended a local community college and graduated magna cum laude with an associate of arts and sciences degree in art and design.

She continues to utilize her cochlear implant on a daily basis. If the person with whom she is communicating is a fluent signer, she continues speaking, rarely communicating solely in sign language. If the person with whom she is communicating has normal hearing, Kyler speaks without signing. She may, however, unconsciously throw out a sign or two on occasion, almost as if to enhance conceptual clarity as one would naturally gesture while speaking.

Finally, a note about capitalization.

In 1972 James Woodward proposed the convention of using the lowercase "deaf" when referring to the audiological condition of not being able to hear and the uppercase "Deaf" when referring to the particular group of people who share a language (e.g., American Sign Language) and a culture. In the following pages, the goal is to follow that convention. However, this text focuses primarily on issues surrounding deaf children born to hearing parents. It highlights a family experience that does not involve enculturation into Deaf culture and the use of ASL. In those cases, "deaf" is utilized. In quoting materials written prior to 1972 and before that distinction was made, I have followed the usage of the particular source. Where a lowercase *d* is used, the information refers to the absence of hearing and does not indicate identification with Deaf culture or the use of ASL. At other times, "d/Deaf" is used, indicating that the information can apply equally to individuals with hearing loss who do not relate to the greater Deaf community and to persons who identify with all that is connected to Deaf culture. As a result, the reader will note a varying use of *deaf, Deaf,* and *d/Deaf* in an effort to differentiate among those divisions.

Chapter 1

Lessons from the Past

Those who do not learn from history are doomed to repeat it.
—GEORGE SANTAYANA, 1863–1952

History That Tells a Story

The chapters that follow tell a story. It is about the birth of a child born deaf, her family, and her successful journey into young adulthood. However, hers is a story within a broader story . . . that of deaf education, the historical challenges of deaf individuals who preceded her and their struggle to escape being marginalized by society. It is only within the context of the larger picture that we can truly appreciate the philosophies that undergird the field of deaf education and understand how they came into being. From there we can begin to comprehend the struggles that hearing parents of deaf children face and the choices they must make as they wade through the decision-making process. They must consider whether to utilize amplification (hearing aids or cochlear implants) to embrace sign language or go with an auditory-oral approach. In addition, they must evaluate the available options and decide what may constitute the most appropriate learning environment for their child.

Whether we are parents of a d/Deaf child or professionals in the field of deafness, we are unable to properly contemplate the needs of the child or student without first becoming familiar with a historical perspective of deafness and how its history has had an effect on the educational processes in use today and the philosophies we currently hold. What follows is a cursory historical introduction to the field of deaf education with an explanation of the influences that continue to shape current philosophies, pedagogies (the science of teaching), educational placements, and curricula.

Evolutionary speculation states that language began first as gesture, gained linguistic meaning, and finally evolved into spoken language (Stokoe, 2001). Ladd (2003) asserts, "It is probable that Deaf people who communicate by gesture or sign have existed as part of humanity from its inception" (p. 296).

It would seem that, from the time humankind has had the ability to set thoughts in writing, the plight and place of deaf individuals has been a topic of consideration. Aristotle is credited with saying, "Those who are born deaf all become senseless and incapable of reason" (355 BC). Deafness is a topic contemplated in Plato's *Cratylus* (360 BC), in which Socrates muses about human intellect and notes that persons born intact, but without speech, give no demonstration of intelligence. He then deduces that deaf people are incapable of generating either language or ideas, concluding they are therefore without intellect. Quite possibly the earliest mention of the rights and privileges of deaf persons was in the Talmud, where Hebrew law provided deaf individuals with limited rights to property and marriage. Although protected from being cursed by others, they were denied full participation in the rituals of the temple (Lane, 1984). Suffice it to say, records from 1000 to 360 BC indicate that deaf persons who had no spoken language were deemed to be less than human.

Such attitudes remained prevalent during the Dark Ages, as is made apparent in an article that appeared in the *New York Times* in the late nineteenth century and titled "The Deaf and Dumb in Antiquity." The author details the experience of deaf people as follows:

> The ancients had the greatest horror of all that was feeble and infirm; with them poverty was despicable and suffering a scandal. It is no wonder then that among the beauty and pleasure-loving Greeks the deaf-mute was looked upon as a disgrace to humanity, and under the barbarous laws of Lycurgus they were exposed to die. Nor was highly cultured Athens less cruel than Sparta toward these unfortunate creatures. Deaf-mute children were pitilessly sacrificed without a voice being raised on their behalf. The Romans treated these unfortunates with the same cruelty as the Greeks. As soon as a child was found to be deaf and dumb, it was sacrificed to the Tiber. (November 2, 1884)

A more enlightened view was a long time coming. The first person of record to teach deaf children was Pedro Ponce de León, a priest who lived in the late 1500s. He spent the better part of the sixteenth century in a monastery in Oña, Spain. Much of his life was devoted to teaching deaf people, as he reported in a document discovered long afterward in the archives at Oña by a Spanish historian named Feijóo:

> I have pupils who were deaf and dumb from birth, sons of great lords and of notable people, whom I have taught to speak, read, write, and reckon; to pray, to assist at the Mass, to know the doctrines of Christianity, and to confess themselves by speech. Some of them learned Latin and some taught Latin and Greek, learned to understand Italian . . . Some were able historians of Spanish and foreign history. Even better, they manifested, by using them, the intellectual faculties that Aristotle denied they could possess. (cited by Lane, 1984, p. 91)

Lane notes in his history of deaf people that the king's historian, who had firsthand account of Ponce de León's teaching methods, reported that the monk taught with signs and writing and that his pupils responded orally. The reason for teaching speech was not primarily religious in nature, nor did Ponce de León believe it was required to cultivate the mind. Rather, it was necessary because a mute person was not considered to be a person at law. Should a family fortune be passed on to a first-born who had not acquired spoken language, the family would lose all (Lane, 1984).

As early as 1521 Rudolf Agricola, a Dutch humanist, believed that deaf people could communicate via writing. He advocated the theory that the ability to speak was separate from the ability to think. During the same period Girolamo Cardano, an Italian physician and mathematician, recognized the ability of deaf people to reason, thus becoming the first to challenge in written argument Aristotle's belief that hearing was a requirement for understanding.

Works by Juan Pablo Bonet and Sir Kenelm Digby recorded the instructional methodologies used by Pedro Ponce de León. Bonet's book, *The Reduction of Letters and the Art of Teaching the Mute to Speak*, was published in 1620. In this early treatise on the education of deaf people, a critical assumption made by Bonet was that thought precedes language (Moores, 1996). Bonet also stressed the importance of activity and what some would now call multisensory learning (Lang, 2003).

The first books published in England on deaf education were titled *Philocopus*, also known as the *Deaf and Dumbe Man's Friend*, and *Chirologia*, or the *Naturall Language of the Hand*, by British physician John Bulwer. Bulwer's books showed the use of manual signs but did not refer to sign language as the language of deaf people. At the dawning of the Age of Enlightenment philosophers such as Locke, Rousseau, and Condillac debated the nature and origin of spoken language, thought, and the language of signs (Lang, 2003).

George Dalgarno (1626–1687) a Scottish intellectual interested in linguistic problems, made the following provocative comment about the use of signs with deaf infants. "There might be 'successful addresses made to a [deaf] child, even in his cradle,' he wrote, if parents had 'but as nimble a hand, as commonly they have a Tongue" (quoted in Lang, 2003, p. 12).

Abbé Charles Michel de l'Epée (1712–1789) founded the first school for deaf children, the Institution Nationale des Sourds-Muets á Paris, after two deaf sisters whose teacher had died were brought to him. He watched them communicate in signs and, through his association with them, became aware of a signing community of two hundred deaf Parisians. It was after this introduction that the priest began instructing deaf children, emphasizing the visual-gestural modality and introducing the use of what he referred to as "methodical signs" (Lanc, 1984; Lang, 2003).

Rousseau took a special interest in examining deaf children instructed by a teacher named Jacobo Pereire, who used pronunciation, signs, fingerspelling, and speechreading. Speechreading, sometimes referred to as lipreading, was thought to assist in the comprehension of spoken language by having the deaf individual attend to and interpret movements of the lips, articulators, and facial expression. Abbé de l'Epée was influenced by Rousseau's emphasis on a "natural" pedagogy. Epée observed deaf children in his school as they utilized natural sign language and allowed them to continue to sign, as he felt it was their nature. He was also influenced by Descartes's semiotic theory, which maintained that a system of signs could exist in which any object could be arbitrarily designated by a sign. The abbot concluded that "system" could and should include manual signs. He enriched the signs with grammatical information specific to spoken French to be used for the purposes of instruction (Lang, 2003).

In the eighteenth century there were two primary schools of thought regarding the education of deaf children. Education that included the use of sign language to convey meaning was referred to as "manualism," whereas instruction that prohibited all use of sign language and relied strictly on lipreading to glean information was known as "oralism."

The European founders of manualism (Epée) and oralism (Samuel Heinicke) exchanged letters expressing their irreconcilable differences on educating deaf students. Thus began the "war of methods" between the proponents of the systematic use of sign language in educating deaf children and those who decried sign language and instead advocated the use of speech, speechreading, and residual hearing as an all-encompassing solution (Lang, 2003, p. 13).

Abbé Roch-Ambroise Cucurron Sicard was Epée's successor at the school for deaf children in Paris. When Napoleon returned to Paris in March 1815, bringing with him the inevitability of war, Sicard decided that he should leave temporarily for reasons of safety. During that time Sicard visited London, bringing with him deaf students Jean Massieu and Laurent Clerc. There the three lectured and demonstrated their teaching methods (Lane, 1984).

Meanwhile, in the United States, the Reverend Thomas Hopkins Gallaudet of Hartford, Connecticut, had been prevailed upon by his friend and neighbor, Dr. Mason Fitch Cogswell, to establish a school for deaf children. Cogswell's desire resulted from the fact that his young daughter, Alice, was herself deaf. Gallaudet was eventually sent to Europe to learn methods of teaching deaf people. Precluded from visiting the famed Braidwood Academy by then headmaster Robert Kinniburgh, who feared that the time-honored oralist methods of teaching deaf children would become familiar to others, Gallaudet looked elsewhere for instruction. It was by a twist of fate that Gallaudet's visit to London coincided with Sicard's stopover. Gallaudet was introduced to Sicard by a member of Parliament. Sicard, in turn, introduced Gallaudet to Clerc and Massieu, and Gallaudet was persuaded to visit their school in Paris. By 1816 Clerc had become Sicard's chief assistant and was teaching the highest class offered at the institution. In addition to his classes with Sicard, Massieu, and Clerc, Gallaudet was also given private lessons by Clerc. Gallaudet was so impressed by Clerc that he invited the "master teacher" to come to the United States to help establish a school for deaf children (Lane, 1984; Lang, 2003).

The history of deaf education in the United States thus began with the founding of the Connecticut Asylum for the Education and Instruction of Deaf and Dumb Persons (now called the American School for the Deaf) in Hartford, Connecticut, in 1817. Clerc and Gallaudet successfully opened the school in Hartford, using a natural sign language developed from the French sign language known by Clerc, combined with natural signs that arose through conversation with the students. Between 1817 and 1855 more than fifteen residential schools for deaf children were established throughout the United States. The primary method of communication in each school was sign language. Nearly four out of every ten teachers in these schools were themselves deaf. Deaf teachers and school administrators were a common phenomenon during that era. It was by way of such schools, as well as Deaf clubs and social organizations, that sign language flourished and Deaf culture became firmly established (Padden & Humphries, 2005).

In 1871 Alexander Graham Bell joined the ranks of those interested in teaching deaf children. His desire was to dispense with sign language and to concentrate instead on the utilization of hearing technology, lipreading, and speech acquisition. His lot was firmly cast in support of the oral philosophy. An international conference held in Milan, Italy, in 1880 aligned the fate of deaf education with the ideals of the oralists, making a mark that has been indelible. Giulio Tarra, an abbot, was selected as president of the conference. He made the following argument in support of oralism:

> Oral speech is the sole power that can rekindle the light God breathed into man when, giving him a soul in a corporeal body, he gave him also a means of understanding, of conceiving, and of expressing himself . . . while, on the one hand, mimic signs are not sufficient to express the fullness of thought, on the other they enhance and glorify fantasy and all the faculties of the sense of imagination . . . The fantastic language of signs exalts the senses and foments the passions, whereas speech elevates the mind much more naturally, with calm, prudence and truth and avoids the danger of exaggerating the sentiment expressed and provoking harmful mental impressions. (Lane, 1984, p. 394)

A vote was taken, and out of the 164 delegates in attendance only the five U.S. representatives (one of whom was deaf) voted against the resolution. Thus the decision was made for oral language to be the language of preference, resulting in an international initiative to bar the use of sign language as a method of communication and hence instruction (Van Cleve & Crouch, 1989).

Abbé Tara later wrote, "All discussions have ceased, serious objections have of themselves disappeared, and the long struggle between systems has ended. Never perhaps has a scientific victory been proclaimed with less opposition" (Lane, 1984, p. 395). Although there remained schools for deaf children in the United States, where sign language continued to be the preferred mode of communication, most of the European schools quickly converted to an oral philosophy, and in slow succession an ever-increasing number of the schools for deaf children in the United States followed suit. By the end of the nineteenth century, oralism would be the philosophy of choice for nearly 40% of the schools for deaf children, increasing to 80% by 1920. As a result, sign language was banished from the classroom. The exclusion of sign language led to a tidal wave of change, resulting in many deaf teachers being exiled from the classroom, as well as administrative positions. The requirement that spoken language be modeled at all times meant that only hearing persons could conduct the business of educating deaf children (Padden & Humphries, 2005).

In the United States, most schools for deaf students were built on property in rural areas or on the outskirts of cities, where deaf children remained out of the public eye. Schools tended to be self-sufficient, often containing their own dairy, vegetable gardens, and orchards. Many schools maintained their own cobbler, bakery, as well as upholstery, carpentry, dry-cleaning, and printing shops, which supplied the needs of faculty, students, and the surrounding community. Because these schools were typically situated in isolated locations and students were often attracted from significant distances, opportunities to visit home were by necessity infrequent. Typically students' ability to visit their families occurred only at Christmas and during the summer. Such a system required each institution to have several dormitories to serve as a residence for the students. Normally one building, with boys and girls separated, housed elementary students. Additional separate dorms were maintained for older boys and girls. Schools for deaf children in Maryland, Virginia, West Virginia, and most southern states were segregated by race, resulting in the establishment of two separate campuses, teaching staffs and administrations (Padden & Humphries, 2005).

It became a common practice for students who had not achieved intelligible speech upon entering high school to then be allowed to sign; as a result, it was permissible for them to receive instruction from deaf teachers. When deaf individuals were removed from positions of authority, they were often hired as houseparents. For many students, deaf houseparents became the source of language learning. Sign language and communication could flourish after hours in the confines of the dormitories, as students signed among themselves as well as any deaf adults with whom they interacted. The controversy that persisted in the nineteenth and twentieth centuries continues to this day. A great deal of the misunderstanding appears to stem from the belief that the language of signs is not a bona fide language but rather a combined use of mime and gesture. In 1960 William Stokoe, professor and chairman of the English Department at Gallaudet University, after viewing reel after reel of videotaped sign language conversations and spending untold hours on their analysis, was able to prove that sign language possessed all of the identifiable characteristics required of a language. Finally, American Sign Language had obtained recognition as a language in its own right, albeit one without a written component. One might think once ASL had been authenticated, the language of signs would have been embraced and the controversy ended. That, however, was not the case (Stokoe, 1960; Lane, 1984).

Philosophies: Oralism/English Only vs. American Sign Language

The history of Deaf education is fraught with conflict; the source of the controversy lies in one's perspective regarding the inability to hear. If one accepts the understanding held by the Deaf community, deafness is viewed through the lens of cultural and linguistic difference. Theirs is the language of signs; hands are the articulators, the air a canvas on which to paint all manner of conversation. Facial expression and body language convey emotion, inflection, and intensity. It is a language of beauty and grace, a language that is inaudible.

The other lens views deafness as a disability, one in need of rehabilitation or medical correction. All educational efforts revolve around the notion of making the deaf child "normal."

From the early technology of the ear trumpet to current digital hearing aids and cochlear implants, the reigning incentive in the auditory/oral movement is to maximize an individual's usable hearing. "Normalcy" is approached as speech discrimination and speech intelligibility improve, and spoken language is fully accessed. This approach, when successful, purports to allow deaf individuals to more fully assimilate into the hearing, speaking mainstream of society.

Due to the fact that a minimum of 90% of all deaf children are born to parents who have normal hearing, one can appreciate the desire to have children communicate in the mode utilized by their family. Hence, many educators and medical professionals advocate an auditory/oral approach, arguing that it is the most logical and desirable of the choices available to families when all other family members have normal hearing. Those espousing an oral philosophy emphasize the acquisition of language and speech through the utilization of amplification (hearing aids or cochlear implants), lipreading, and auditory training to improve speech-discrimination skills. Ongoing speech therapy, audiological follow-up, and curricular emphasis on vocabulary and language acquisition are critical in order for a sense of auditory/oral "normalcy" to be attained. (Davis, 1974; Geers, Kuehn, & Moog, 1981; Levitt, McGarr, & Geffner, 1987; Moeller et al., 1986; Svirsky et al., 2000).

Findings from a study of factors that contribute to auditory, speech, language, and reading outcomes in children with prelingual deafness after 4 to 6 years of multichannel cochlear implant use indicate that the use of sign communication with these children did not promote auditory and speech skill development and did not result in improvement in overall English language competence (Geers, 2002).

However, findings of more recent studies yield very different results. Giezen (2011) indicates that not only do hard of hearing and deaf children learn more words by the application of signs combined with spoken or written words, but in addition they have greater retention of vocabulary when sign supported speech is utilized. Giezen's research further indicates when signs support spoken words, they do not hinder the auditory speech perception in children with cochlear implants. To the contrary, in the perception of spoken words as well as with reading comprehension students appear to benefit from bimodal input (Spencer, Gantz, & Knutson, 2004). Knoors and Marschark (2012) believe that it is worthwhile to encourage parents of children with cochlear implants and digital hearing aids to learn and use sign language, especially as a support to spoken language. They indicate that signs will support the auditory perception of speech, contribute to language comprehension, and add to an already improved spoken language vocabulary.

American Sign Language is a distinct alternative to oralism and is considered by many to be the natural language of Deaf persons. Proponents of ASL recognize sight as being the most useful sense the Deaf person has for receiving information. ASL is a visual-spatial language that uses handshape, location, and movement; body language; gestures; facial expressions; and other visual cues to convey meaning. It has its own morphology and syntax, which are distinct from English (Fant, 1972). American Sign Language is most often the first language for Deaf children born to Deaf parents (who use ASL), as well as for many hearing children born to Deaf parents. While ASL is a viable and rich language in its own right, its detractors point out that it cannot be reduced to written form and as such has no carryover to written or spoken English, a language based on the relationship between sounds and their alphabetic symbol counterparts. Its proponents, however, would argue that, in a bilingual educational setting, ASL promotes the acquisition of written English.

This, then, is the current educational state of d/Deaf children who have available to them a variety of means by which to communicate and learn. In many ways multiple options compound the decision-making process making it more, not less, difficult for parents to predict which approach/es will best meet the needs of their child. This was certainly the case with Kyler's parents as they pondered the communication and education choices available to them in 1989 (the year Kyler's deafness was identified) and the years immediately thereafter. It was against a backdrop of differing ideological and educational placement perspectives and the quite recent (at that time) access to cochlear implants that they wrestled with the decisions of how to proceed in the best interests of their daughter.

Chapter 2

Freedom to Thrive

Pedagogies: Oppression vs. Liberation

In 1992 Harlan Lane published his second book on deafness, *The Mask of Benevolence: Disabling the Deaf Community*. The title says it all and raises the question of the motive behind one's choice to work with a marginalized population. Some may be familiar with a stage play by Mark Medoff that was later made into a movie, *Children of a Lesser God*. The crux of the play is a romance between a hearing speech teacher of deaf students and his interaction with a recent deaf graduate at a school for deaf people. The goal of the speech therapist/teacher is to give voice to deaf people, to teach students who cannot hear how to acquire intelligible speech. The speech therapist and the young deaf woman, both recent employees at the school, develop an odd alliance, eventually fall in love, and marry. The speech therapist/ husband encourages his wife to attempt to acquire spoken communication. He becomes angry and perplexed at her refusal, a choice he feels limits her. She responds by intimating that he merely pities her rather than attempting to understand her perspective. At one point in an argument, she uses her voice to satisfy his wish for her to do so. The resulting change from the silence of signs to shrill, ear-piercing sounds emitted through constricted vocal cords is gripping. Her voice, so startling and jarring, leaves all who hear its pained expression wondering about the scars left on the Deaf children of the world because of the demand that they speak. Her voice is that of one who is unable to modulate pitch, quality, or volume. It becomes the collective voice of Deaf people, begging to be accepted as they are, pleading not to be forced to accommodate individuals who would impose a philosophical perspective that regards spoken language as superior.

Who could not help but admire—nay, even wish to emulate—the teacher? Who could not think that the awakening of the tongue is less than the noblest of all tasks? And with those desires, intrinsically good, is there not the potential to view students as recipients of a teacher's beneficence? Such notions, notwithstanding an element of altruism and decency, contain an opportunity for what Paulo Freire (2007) terms the banking concept of education, in which

> knowledge is a gift bestowed by those who consider themselves knowledgeable upon those whom they consider to know nothing. Projecting an absolute ignorance onto others, a characteristic of the ideology of oppression, negates education and knowledge as processes of inquiry. The teacher presents himself to his students as their necessary opposite; by considering their ignorance absolute, he justifies his own existence. (p. 72)

According to Freire, reconciliation of the matter can occur only when both parties are simultaneously students and teachers: "To impede communication is to reduce men to the status of things" (p. 128), a quote bearing much significance for the Deaf population.

The Merriam-Webster dictionary defines "oppressed" as meaning "to crush or burden by abuse of power or authority." Paulo Freire sees the great humanistic and historical task of the oppressed to be that of liberating themselves and their oppressors as well (p. 44). He notes that many oppressed people have a fear of freedom as it requires one to assume the mantle of self-determination and responsibility. How should one acquire freedom? Freire believes one does so by conquest and advises that initiation of the struggle for freedom is difficult because oppressed people have become resigned to their situation, not to mention that their efforts may well result in even greater oppression. It involves taking immense risk and convincing others to do the same.

Like childbirth, liberation is painful. Freire looks with disdain upon those who speak of the worthiness of all humanity and yet do nothing to resolve issues of oppression. "To affirm that men and women are persons and as persons should be free, and yet to do nothing tangible to make this affirmation a reality, is a farce" (p. 50). Oppression is viewed as a form of domestication, whose crush can be removed only by reflection and change. Freire's notion of righting this wrong is most interesting in that he acknowledges that the sword of freedom has a most beneficial double edge. It liberates oppressed people and restores to the oppressors the humanity lost in the exercise of oppression (p. 56). Freire makes clear the idea that a simple role reversal does not, indeed cannot, alleviate the crises.

The battle for civil rights among the African American population has inspired many marginalized groups and individuals to follow the demand for equality, among them, the Deaf community. "The Civil Rights movement has given great impetus to the belief that minorities should define themselves and that minority leaders should have a significant say in the conduct of minority affairs" (Lane, Hoffmeister, & Bahan, 1996, p. 447).

On March 6, 1988, Gallaudet University's Board of Trustees announced that a hearing person had been selected as Gallaudet's seventh president. It is important to note that the previous six presidents were also persons with normal hearing. In the months (or, by some accounts, the years) leading up to the appointment, many in the Deaf community advocated for a Deaf person to be named to the presidency. Two of the three finalists for the position were Deaf; hence many people assumed that the next president of Gallaudet would be a Deaf person.

Despite the strongly held desire among the Gallaudet student body, faculty, and the Deaf community at large for a Deaf person to fill the position, the board chose the only hearing candidate, Elisabeth Zinser. Frustrated with the decision, Gallaudet students, supported by a number of alumni, faculty, and staff, shut down the campus.

The students and their supporters then submitted the following four demands to the Board of Trustees:

1. Elisabeth Zinser must resign, and a deaf person must be selected as president.
2. Jane Spilman must step down as chairperson of the Board of Trustees.
3. Deaf people must constitute a 51% majority on the board.
4. No reprisals would be enacted against any student or employee involved in the protest.

By the end of the week, Dr. I. King Jordan had been selected as Gallaudet's eighth—and its first deaf—president (Gannon, 1989; Calderon & Greenberg, 2003; Leigh & Pollard, 2003).

In her book *Disabling Pedagogy: Power, Politics, and Deaf Education*, Linda Komesaroff (2002) applies Freire's notion of oppression to the current condition of Deaf people in Australia. She indicates that their plight is more than loss of privilege; it is in addition a loss of the ability to access language. Language is more than a form of communication; it connects us to our cultural heritage, allows for freedom of expression and the exchange of ideas, and in a very real sense is part of our identity. Helen Keller once stated, "The problems of deafness are deeper and more complex, if not more important than those of blindness. Deafness is a much worse misfortune. For it means the loss of the most vital stimulus—the sound of the voice that brings language, sets thoughts astir, and keeps us in the intellectual company of man. Blindness separates us from things, but deafness separates us from people" (1905).

Komesaroff notes, "A cultural view of deafness does not confuse *language* with *speech* and challenges the assumption that deafness is a barrier to learning" (2002, p. 4). Often speech is considered to be synonymous with language; however, in reality one can have language without having the ability to speak. Conversely, it is impossible to have spoken communication without first having language. "Keeping native sign language out of the classroom or assigning it a subordinate role are examples of the way in which schools put learners at risk by erecting barriers to learning" (Cambourne, 1990, quoted in Komesaroff, 2002, p. 291). This position ignores the legitimacy of native sign languages and illustrates the way in which a minority language and its users can be rendered invisible" (Komesaroff, 2002, p. 4). Komesaroff's point is that when sign language is the preferred mode of communication, deafness need not become the barrier to which Helen Keller alludes.

Such perspectives allow one to easily equate the circumstances of a population who cannot hear with others who have been disenfranchised. Freire acknowledges that it is only when one assumes the existence of the oppressed and becomes a comrade, that understanding of ways of living and behaving can occur. Until such a transition has occurred, there is merely an attempt to cure ills from the perspective of an outsider. Decisions regarding the needs of marginalized populations typically are not made by those groups but rather by those in power. In the case of Deaf people, decisions about how they were to be taught and how they were to communicate were most often made by hearing leaders who frequently could not communicate with the signing Deaf population (Komesaroff, 2002).

Currently schools for deaf students are shrinking in size, and many are being permanently closed as a result of the interpretation of Public Law 94-142, or the Education for All Handicapped Children Act. The law was passed in order to accomplish four major goals: (1) to ensure that special education services are available to children who need them; (2) to guarantee that decisions about services for students with disabilities are fair and appropriate; (3) to establish specific management and auditing requirements for special education; and (4) to provide federal funds to help states educate students with disabilities. In addition, PL 94-142 contains a provision that these students should be placed in the "least restrictive environment," that is, one that allows the greatest opportunity to interact with students without impairments. Separate schooling may occur only when the nature or severity of the disability is such that instructional goals cannot be achieved in the regular classroom.

Many people view the separate schooling of d/Deaf and hard of hearing students as a more (or perhaps the most) restrictive environment. This kind of thinking has endangered the existence of schools for Deaf students. In such a climate, what will become of Deaf culture? Will the opportunity for d/Deaf and hard of hearing children to learn from d/Deaf teachers, mentors, and role models become forever lost? Consider as well the opportunity for interacting and developing meaningful relationships with peers; will that too become a casualty of the current wave of what is considered to be progressive thinking?

Of additional concern to those who embrace Deaf culture is the announcement in 2003 by the National Institutes of Health (NIH) that the sequencing of the human genome has been completed. The NIH reported that the Human Genome Project was able to identify almost thirty thousand genes, including those involved in genetic deafness. With the ability to isolate genetic deafness comes the concern that deafness will be targeted as a defect to be eliminated.

Padden and Humphries (2005) point out that sign language is now more widely embraced than ever before and that many high schools and universities are offering courses in American Sign Language. Does it not seem a conflict, on the one hand, to acknowledge the beauty of diversity, while on the other to try to "fix" those considered to be of defective genetic construction so that all are made "normal"? It seems an incredible dilemma. Padden and Humphries (ibid.) query why it is that bilingualism is considered normal, even desirable, in hearing children, yet that is not the case with Deaf children.

Arnos and Pandya, who wrote a chapter in the *Oxford Handbook of Deaf Studies: Language and Education,* titled "Advances in the Genetics of Deafness (2003), note that geneticists have estimated that approximately half of the cases of deafness at birth or in early childhood can be traced to genetic causes, with the remaining cases caused by illness, such as meningitis. Conceivably we are fast approaching the time when a couple can be screened for genetic deafness and potentially be given the choice of altering their child's genetic makeup or choosing not to bear children. Will society then be able to genetically engineer all progeny so as to eliminate traits considered undesirable?

With such social uncertainties and educational concerns, the field of deaf education finds itself atop a precipice. Lane, Hoffmeister, and Bahan (1996) note that obstacles to replacing a disability construction of Deaf people with a language-minority construction are daunting. They suggest that collaboration is possible if all parties involved show mutual respect for each party's language and culture. Such a collaborative effort is at the crux of a more recent philosophical approach to deaf education known as a bilingual/bimodal model, or BiBi, as it has come to be called. Since 1990 there has been a shift toward the ASL/English bilingual approach to education of deaf children. In this approach teachers in the schools serving Deaf and hard of hearing children are expected to use ASL as the language of instruction and teach English through reading and writing rather than require children to learn to speak or to use a Signed English system (Simms & Thumann, 2007). Researchers propose that a bilingual approach provides a potential means of surmounting the linguistic and educational barriers that are faced by Deaf and hard of hearing children and establishes a bilingual perspective (Johnson, Liddell, & Erting, 1989). Grosjean (1992) stresses the significance of the continued study of Deaf bilingualism, the importance of Deaf people realizing that they are indeed bilingual, and finally the necessity of bringing up Deaf children bilingually, with sign language as their primary language and the majority language as a second language.

Curricular Implications

Curriculum refers to what actually happens in a learning environment. The intended and real curricula are products of a dynamic and complex network of relationships between people and a wide diversity of influences, including implicit and explicit, human and physical (Cohen & Harrison, 1982). There is significant potential for some of the values that underpin the curriculum to be unstated and taken for granted, allowing what has been called the "hidden curriculum" to surface. The hidden curriculum refers to unplanned and usually unrecognized learning outcomes that occur as a consequence of the curriculum (Power & Leigh, 2003). "Many of the messages of the hidden curriculum are concerned with power, authority, access and participation: these are messages that continually shape learners' developing views of the world . . . their creating of reality" (Lovat & Smith, 1998, pp. 35–36). This raises questions about what the dominant perspective or ideology of those professionals who design curricula might be and whether they reflect all or only some constructions of reality for d/Deaf and hard of hearing people (Power & Leigh, 2003).

Differences in pedagogical perspectives discussed previously cannot help but play a role in influencing curriculum context. From an audiologist's point of view, deafness may be defined in terms of degree, etiology, and age of onset. From a developmental perspective there will be a focus on the impact that varying degrees of hearing loss may have on language and speech development, including mode of communication, social-emotional development, and whether there are coexisting developmental disabilities. In addition, there is the potential for a legal or policy perspective, a medical perspective, or a sociocultural perspective on deafness, each one of which carries its own associated parameters for definition and description (Padden & Humphries, 1988; Power, 1997; Taylor & Bishop, 1991; Woll & Ladd, 2003; Power & Leigh, 2003).

The principal beliefs on which deafness is defined and perceived by those who control the processes of curriculum development and implementation will affect its focus. If, for example, an early intervention program is developed based on the dominant medical and audiological perspective, the curriculum context will be one in which the child is seen only as a member of the broader community with a communication disability in need of being ameliorated. By the same token, if the dominant perspective is of a sociocultural nature, the curriculum context will be one where the primary cultural affiliation is with the Deaf community and the development of sign language is seen to be of preeminent importance, possibly with no emphasis on spoken language development (Power & Leigh, 2003).

As Leigh points out:

> To fail to acknowledge that a particular perspective on deafness may lead to the adoption of a set of objectives for a deaf student that are not consonant with that student's current or

future social circumstances may result in a situation where both educational means and ends are subsequently questioned or rejected by that student and his or her cultural community. There are, for example, unfortunate examples of young deaf students and deaf adults who have come to question, often bitterly, the lack of inclusion of sign language and deaf culture in their educational experiences (Jacobs, 1994). Similarly, some deaf people educated in more socioculturally defined programs have come to question their lack of access to assistive technologies for hearing and their lack of programmed opportunity to develop expressive spoken language skills (Bertling, 1994). Clearly, there are issues relating to current and future cultural affiliation that must be considered in curriculum design. (2001, pp. 158–59)

Stewart and Kluwin (2001) report that more than four out of every five students with hearing loss are educated in regular mainstream schools, either in regular classrooms or special classes within regular schools. With that being the case, the influence of the general curriculum and the need to conform to general curriculum standards is increasing (Moores, 2001). As Power and Leigh (2003) note, effective curriculum design for d/Deaf students involves determining additional or alternative educational objectives and experiences required to achieve the same overall outcomes as for other students. They believe the following issues related to the development of a first language for d/Deaf and hard of hearing students should be matters of consideration:

- The possibility that children from certain ethnic, linguistic, or racial minorities may be overrepresented in the d/Deaf school-age population (Lynas & Turner, 1995; Schildroth & Hotto, 1996)
- The potential for significant differences between d/Deaf and hearing learners with regard to their organization of knowledge and their long- and short-term memory processes (Marschark, 1993)

- The frequently considerable difference between the language and communication skills of d/Deaf children and others in their daily environments (Gallaway, 1998; Marschark, Lang, & Albertini, 2002)
- The possibility that d/Deaf students will have limited vocabularies and a restricted range of meanings for words with multiple meanings (Geers & Schick, 1988; McEvoy, Marschark, & Nelson, 1999)
- The potential that the d/Deaf learners' preferred language will be sign language, requiring the use of interpreters for educational purposes (Messenheimer-Young & Whitesell, 1995), as well as the limitations of interpreting as a basis for equitable access to classroom communication (Innes, 1994; Lang, 2002; Seal, 1998; Watson & Parsons, 1998)
- The often significant discrepancy between the levels of reading and writing ability of d/Deaf students and their hearing peers, with increasing inequity as they progress through school (Traxler, 2000)
- The physical and mental demands on d/Deaf students, who have to simultaneously take in ongoing communications and other visual sources of information, such as computer screens and overhead projection devices. Such impositions on their awareness require constant switching of visual attention. Hearing learners do not have to contend with these obstacles (Matthews & Reich, 1993; Wood et al., 1986).

For the most part, children come to school with first-language skills in place. However, for d/Deaf students no such assumption can be made. As a result, a language curriculum component holds key importance for d/Deaf and hard of hearing students. For them, language development has been expanded from a term that typically refers to monolingual language acquisition to one that may include the acquisition of language bimodally, as is the case with spoken/written and signed language (Luetke-Stahlman, 1998). Language objectives in a curriculum may relate to the development of a spoken language and/or a signed language in one or more modes of communication, including spoken language and/or signs and visual symbols represented in one or more modes of communication that can be spoken, signed, cued, and written (Power & Leigh, 2003).

Implications

In looking at pedagogical implications that may be gleaned from historical, philosophical, and curricular understandings, Harry Lang (2003) notes several important considerations. Today, possibly more than at any other time in the history of education, we recognize the importance of parental involvement in both formal and informal educational endeavors. In particular are the studies demonstrating the long-term influence of mother-child relationships, early communication, and the need to provide d/Deaf children with a variety of experiences during the early years.

Other emerging considerations include the importance of examining educational history in ways that include the many incidences of d/Deaf persons taking control of and influencing the field of d/Deaf education. It is not uncommon for hearing writers to give critical reference to methodologies and philosophies while neglecting to "examine how d/Deaf people have overcome barriers in many periods of history under a wide variety of conditions to make important contributions in education and other fields" (Lang, 2003, p. 18). Such an inclusion of study for teachers preparing to become teachers of d/Deaf children and for d/Deaf students themselves would provide rich biographical resources and give insight into the wide range of accomplishments of d/Deaf people. Studies of this nature would go a long way toward eliminating the pedagogical lens of deafness as a disability. It would also allow teachers of d/Deaf children to see all that is within their students' grasp.

Historical research in the field of d/Deaf education yields a multitude of practices that have generated evidence-based results, many of which have been lost or discarded over time. Those include utilization of metacognitive skills to enhance the reading process and critical devotion to reading in order to access the curriculum. Such applications were utilized extensively a century ago but seem to have dropped out of sight under the authority of federal guidelines and mandates (Public Law 94-142 and No Child Left Behind) that have influenced educational placement and support scripted teaching methodologies. Lang (2003) calls for comprehensive analyses of perspectives on issues such as standardized testing, the relationships between memory and reading, the construction of learning experiences through enculturation, and the impact of stigmatizing Deaf people by viewing deafness as a disability.

Possibly the most agonizing lesson to learn is that of recognizing individuality in students who arrive at our educational institutions. During the last half of the twentieth century educators began to replace the formerly held view of d/Deaf children as concrete, literal thinkers with a more thorough understanding of the interactions of language and intellectual development. Research is conclusive with regard to the necessity of early access to meaningful language in order to achieve normal cognitive development and academic success for both d/Deaf and hearing children. "The complexity and sometimes contradictory nature of findings emphasize the need for care in evaluating language development, cognitive growth, and academic achievement, and they reinforce the importance of recognizing that these factors are rarely independent" (Lang, 2003, p. 19). In light of knowledge about d/Deaf learners that we have gained during the past several decades, the current century should be distinguished by comprehensive research and meaningful instruction, appropriate curriculum development, and programming.

What can we learn from a review of historical, philosophical, and pedagogical perspectives? Foremost would seem to be that philosophical and pedagogical battles concerning how d/Deaf children should be taught have been waged for centuries. It seems that we are no closer to achieving consensus on the matter than we were at the first pondering of how d/Deaf children are best able to learn language. Secondly, it is readily apparent that much time, energy, and emotion have been spent supporting the consideration of speech over sign language and vice versa or a combination of the two. The lines of division continue to be drawn among these schools of thought, leading one to ponder what, if anything, could be learned should hearts, minds, and purpose be joined.

There is an incredible body of research and literature available addressing the historical aspects of deaf education, family education, early language development, and processes of teaching d/Deaf children, so much so that one might consider assimilating the whole of it an impossible task. That said, it should become the lifetime endeavor of all who choose to become teachers of d/Deaf students. Failure to be fully aware of the historical context of d/Deaf people and to be knowledgeable of the issues effecting d/Deaf children and their families is unconscionable. Neglecting to consider all of the options available to d/Deaf children and their families simply continues to promote the "either/or" mentality that has prevailed to date. It seems that most often teachers embrace one philosophy at the expense of another at the outset of teacher preparation, and the rest of their preparation and teaching career is spent justifying a given method or approach rather than other available options.

One must question whether the entrenchment observed in the schools of thought regarding how to best teach d/Deaf and hard of hearing children has benefited those who are the supposed beneficiaries. As with higher education in general, a delicate balance must be achieved between knowledge that is a mile wide and an inch deep and the equally inappropriate inch-wide and mile-deep programs of study. One can only ponder the impact that teachers exposed to varying schools of thought in equal doses might have on the populations of future students they will teach. To assume that all children learn in the same way, at the same time, using the same modalities, whether hearing, d/Deaf, or hard of hearing, seems absurd, and yet that is precisely what a prescriptive philosophy presupposes. The assumption that children with varying degrees of hearing loss and etiologies should best learn in an environment whose accommodations have been predetermined or preset based on an assumed philosophy and/or pedagogy raises the question of the purpose of having an individualized educational program.

Families of newly identified d/Deaf children can benefit from this review of the struggles and perspectives within the field of Deaf education to better understand the whys of current educational practices. Additionally, and above all else, parents and caregivers should feel free to move forward in pursuit of an educational/philosophical choice that best meets the needs of their child rather than being coerced into accepting an "either/ or" prescriptive educational approach.

Imagine the potential for learning if specialized schools were to be established that housed professionals from various educational persuasions whose stated objective was to observe, evaluate, and work collaboratively with the children and families they serve to determine the best ways to facilitate learning. One can only imagine the possibilities that might be realized.

Chapter 3

Field of Dreams

I have spread my dreams under your feet; Tread softly because you tread on my dreams.

—WILLIAM BUTLER YEATS, "HE WISHES
FOR THE CLOTHS OF HEAVEN"

Parents of newborn babies greet their children with hopes, dreams, and grand expectations. Among the approximately 4.13 million annual births in the United States, the Department of Health and Human Services reports that approximately 5% are children who have a hearing loss sufficient to impede speech and language acquisition. It is not uncommon for hearing parents, upon learning of their child's deafness, to experience a strong emotional reaction to the clinical pronouncement. Their dreams have not only been trod upon; they have, in some cases, been shattered. Parents may deny the deafness itself, the condition of being deaf regarding its permanence, or the reality of the impact deafness will have on their child's communication and socialization as they begin to attempt to understand their child's inability to hear.

Most often hearing parents experience feelings of sadness, disappointment, hurt, guilt, embarrassment, shame, blame, anger, bewilderment, and/or a sense of isolation upon learning of their child's deafness. Such feelings can distort parents' perceptions of their children and interfere with their ability to process all of the advice and information that are suddenly thrust upon them.

It is not uncommon for tension within the family to arise should the parents be in differing stages in coming to grips with the situation at hand (Calderon & Greenberg, 1997, 1999; Ferris, 1980; Mindel & Vernon, 1971).

Author and cochlear implant recipient Michael Chorost describes the shock as follows:

> For parents, a child's handicap often causes a grieving not incomparable to that following death. Every parent prayerfully imagines their child's first steps, bat mitzvah or first communion, first date, graduation, marriage, and beyond, and their hopes range ever forward into that vague future in which they find their own grave but not their child's. But when their child cannot see, or hear, or walk, those multifold futures die. They can no longer see their child as a strong, confident, proud adult. In its place they see nightmare images of wheelchairs, white canes, hearing aids, halting speech and lifelong dependency. My mother and father walked around for days in sick horror. (p. 28)

It is imperative for parents of d/Deaf children and professionals in the field to appreciate some of the likely psychological ramifications of learning that a child born or adopted into the family is deaf. Dr. McCay Vernon (Mindel & Vernon, 1971) was among the first to isolate the emotions that hearing parents may experience upon first learning of their child's deafness, as well as the process of coming to accept and deal with its implications. Initial reaction to an occurrence of something not expected is that of shock or disbelief. Disbelief can eventually manifest itself as denial. Once deafness is suspected, parents' observations of their child become acutely attuned to watching for a response to auditory stimuli . . . some indication that hearing is indeed present. For instance, loud sounds often produce an accompanying vibratory stimulus like the beating of a drum. In other situations a visual cue or movement can accompany a sound. Given these conditions a child will often respond by looking toward the movement or the source of the vibration. Such behaviors can cause a parent to reason that the child is attending to the sound rather than the vibration or movement, making it more difficult to accept the reality of deafness. However, once irrefutable confirmation of the child's hearing loss occurs, it is not uncommon for parents to experience symptoms of shock.

Shock in this instance, according to Dr. Vernon, is a blend of disbelief and grief, helplessness, anger, and guilt. We are all familiar with the age-old "Why me?" question when what we least expect becomes our reality. Parents may look at others with seemingly perfect children and mourn the loss of what they had envisioned . . . dreams they fear are now lost to them and to their child. As one might imagine, these same feelings may occur when parents who are Deaf give birth to an infant with normal hearing.

Hearing parents of deaf children may have a tendency to over-identify with their child's hearing loss. However, a child deaf from birth does not experience deafness as a loss in terms of having once had hearing and then losing it. Parents, through a sense of empathy, may transpose their own understanding of the loss of hearing and the pleasures they personally enjoy from a variety of auditory experiences onto their child. They may perceive deafness as isolating with regard to its potential impact on communication and resulting social isolation. Families need to recognize, address, and resolve such deep emotions and fears in order to move forward to establish a bond of love and acceptance and, as a result, provide a nurturing environment for their child.

The Dilemmas of Deafness

As mentioned in chapter 1, the most prevalent difficulty in the field of deaf education and among parents of newly identified d/Deaf children is that of coping with the various philosophical models for early intervention and education. When persons and entities like educators of deaf children, public school systems, schools for deaf students, audiologists, and, most recently, otolaryngologists adopt one philosophy exclusive of all others, parents of d/Deaf children—and d/Deaf children themselves—are the ones who lose as a result of the polarization.

Some parents have been informed by surgeons who perform cochlear implant surgeries that, if they want their deaf child to learn to discriminate spoken language and to acquire intelligible speech, they must refrain from using sign language. The notion is that learning a visual-spatial language will impede attention to and development of spoken language. While surgeons and/or audiologists rarely have a background in deaf education, they are often the first professionals with whom families come into contact. As a result of advice from a member of the medical community, parents (without adequate information regarding their child's learning needs) often adopt a philosophy and pursue educational programming that may or may not result in linguistic, academic, and/or psychosocial success.

It is impossible not to find such a dilemma laden with moral and ethical considerations. Having previously served as a faculty member of schools for deaf children and public school mainstream programs for deaf and hard of hearing students, I have witnessed much growth and change within the field of deaf education. Unfortunately, there has been no end to the conflicting perspectives on where deaf children should be educated (schools for deaf children vs. public school placement) or how they should be taught. Although cochlear implants are thought to be a godsend by many audiologists, educators, parents, and implant recipients, scores of Deaf adults, as well as professionals within the field, view implants as a new form of cultural and linguistic genocide.

As parents of deaf children wade through the decision-making process in determining what is best for their child, they are often bombarded with a plethora of conflicting information provided by a variety of well-meaning professionals. Should they (1) opt for a hearing aid or cochlear implant and focus solely on auditory/oral language and communication methodologies; (2) embrace American Sign Language, eschew all forms of amplification, and become fully immersed in Deaf culture; or (3) choose a combination of elements from each school of thought that would enhance learning while allowing everyone involved to benefit from a bilingual lifestyle?

Former colleague and author Caren Ferris (1980) recorded the following comment made by a parent. It clearly expresses the frustration felt regarding the philosophical divide: "Unfortunately, there is a stupid fight going on among the professionals. Some advocate an oral approach to communication. Others support the total approach. Both sides are deeply biased, and I suspect neither knows what the other is doing. The losers are the children. We parents are caught in the middle. We have to decide about our child's future and his education" (p. 28).

In the year 2000, researchers from Gallaudet University published the results of a parent survey. It is disheartening to note that, despite the passing of 20 years (from the time Ferris wrote her book in 1980 until the parent survey in 2000), parents' frustration regarding issues of methodology remains the same. The following quote from the parent of a deaf child cited in the results of the Gallaudet survey echoes the parental dissatisfaction with the methodological entrenchment among professionals in the field of deaf education:

I think . . . when the child is first diagnosed, you feel like all the control has been ripped out of your hands. Everything is now in someone else's hands, and the most important thing seems to be to give some element of control or choice, maybe choice is a better word, some element of choice back to the parent and also to the children, so the parents feel like no one's treating them like a child. I would much rather have been given, just inundated with all this information of different methodologies, different things so we could see how the children track. I mean one [child] might do better with one method and one might do better with another and allowing the families to have more information I think would make the families then more flexible, but everybody's educated in their field to such an extent that they feel like their methodology is the best. And it's kinda what we ran into . . . is we were spoken to in a real condescending manner when we would suggest something different than what they were offering. It was like they didn't want to adapt anything or change any of their services or their methods to accommodate something a little different. (Mertens, Sass-Lehrer, & Scott-Olson, 2000, p. 145)

In response to these charges, professionals in the fields of deaf education, audiology, and otolaryngology should feel obliged to act in a way that encourages parents to explore and utilize the methods of communication, instruction, and support that best meet their child's needs. By the same token, teacher training programs need to incorporate content knowledge, experience, and expertise of various methodologies in their curricula for teachers of d/Deaf and hard of hearing children.

The Importance of Early Detection and Stimulation

Professionals often add to parents' dilemma of which philosophical model to choose for their child, the critical need to make an informed decision, and to do so quickly. Decisions such as these most often result in life-changing consequences over the lifetime of the deaf child and as such require the need to be fully informed before committing to an option exclusive of all others.

The importance of early stimulation during the first three years of life has been well documented. Scientists and neuroscientists have determined that when an infant or young child is stimulated via sound, whether listening to conversation, music, a story, or a nursery rhyme, neural pathways in the brain are being activated. Powerful technologies such as magnetic resonance imaging (MRI) and positron emission tomography (PET) allow scientists to see areas of the brain light up when a stimuli is presented. They are able to witness the firing of neurons as an infant's brain is being wired via experiences presented through sensory stimulation, whether sight, sound, taste, smell, or touch. Neuroscience journalist Jennifer Kahn (2012) observes that "Ninety percent of a young child's knowledge is attributable to hearing background conversation. More than a third of children with even slight hearing loss, researchers estimate, will fail at least one grade"(p. 7).

When I was studying to be a speech pathologist in the early 1970s, a commonly held view was that there was a "critical period" for language acquisition. It was thought that the brain was best able to learn language during a given time frame and, once that had been exceeded, language learning would become increasingly difficult, if not impossible, with little likelihood of mastery.

Eric Lenneberg (1969) hypothesized that human language acquisition is an example of biologically constrained learning and is normally acquired during a critical period, beginning early in life and ending at puberty. He believed that, outside this time period, language could be acquired only with great difficulty. In relation to language acquisition, the term *critical period* is sometimes interpreted as an abrupt decline in the brain's plasticity, resulting in an instantaneous halt with regard to the ability to learn language. More recently the term *sensitive period* has been used to indicate a more gradual loss of brain plasticity, specifically as it relates to language acquisition. The term *sensitive period* indicates a gradual diminishing of the brain's ability to learn language rather than an abrupt halt.

Implications of a "Sensitive Period" for a Child Born with a Significant Hearing Loss

In a series of "critical period" studies of deaf language learners, Rachel Mayberry (1998) found that those who learned sign language as their first language, between the ages of 5 and 19, were specifically affected in the area of grammatical morphology: late learners tend to struggle with word constructions and lexical knowledge (the relationship between words). In terms of syntax, late learners often use sentence constructions that do not follow grammatically correct word order.

Additionally, Mayberry's findings indicate that late language learners tend to misunderstand or forget sentence meaning. Deaf subjects who learned little or no language prior to learning both English and ASL at the same time performed poorly on grammatical judgment and syntactic comprehension tasks and had difficulty understanding complex sentence structures. Mayberry's data led her to conclude that there is clear evidence of a critical period for sign language acquisition and that failure to learn sign language within that period will result in effects that are permanent. She also postulates, based on the results of her studies, that strong parallels exist between the critical period for the development of the visual system and the development of the linguistic system. Persons born with congenital cataracts that prevent them from obtaining visual experience in early childhood grow up to be functionally blind even after the cataracts are successfully removed (e.g., Sacks, 1993). Mayberry concludes, "Our research shows that individuals who are born deaf and isolated from language during early childhood grow up being linguistically dysfunctional" (1998, p. 8).

In an online interview (2011), Dr. David Steinberg, director of the Infancy and Early Childhood Program at the NYU Study

Center and assistant professor of clinical psychiatry at the NYU School of Medicine, notes the following developmental patterns of normal language learning:

> Language development does have peaks and plateaus. Between the ages of 8 months and 3 years a child's language comprehension and strategies become more sophisticated. For example, an 8-month-old understands a few single words and will look at an object when directed verbally, whereas a 3-year-old understands a 3-word sentence. With respect to expressive vocabulary, in spite of individual variation, a 3-year-old has a vocabulary of approximately 900 words, a threefold increase from the amount at age 2.

Steinberg concludes his comments on language acquisition by saying, "Children are best able to learn a new language when they're young." Even though Dr. Steinberg is referring to language development in the child with normal hearing, parallels among d/Deaf and hard of hearing children must be comparable to milestones for hearing children if we are to expect normal intellectual and academic development to follow.

Simply put, the absence of experiences that stimulate the brain during critical or sensitive periods can have a lasting impact. Scientific research shows that young children's brains have optimal periods of development for functions such as visual acuity and language acquisition. The number of brain connections, or synapses, the child's brain makes depends on the variety and richness of the early learning experiences to which babies and toddlers are exposed. Brain cell connections, strengthened through consistent sensory stimulation from the environment, lay the foundation for future achievement in life and success in school.

Speech pathologists, neuroscientists, and psycholinguists agree that the critical or sensitive period for language acquisition begins at birth and continues approximately until the age of 6. Delays in accessible language stimulation may well result in a lifelong struggle to gain linguistic competence. In light of this, decisions about amplification, communication methods, and philosophies are not ones that can be postponed. Stimulation is critical, and accessible communication is vital whether it be auditory/verbal, signed, or a combination of the two. Time is of the essence.

Impact of Deafness on Language Acquisition

Ludwig Wittgenstein, an Austrian philosopher (1922 p. 88), noted, "The limits of my language means the limits of my world." Language is the mechanism that allows for the formulation of thoughts, feelings, hopes, and ideas. Communication, on the other hand, is the vehicle that transmits or conveys those ideas, wants, and needs to others by a systematic means that includes speech, signs, gestures, pictures, and so on. Late nineteenth-century philosopher, Josiah Royce concluded that "without language . . . there would be no self" (quoted in Siegel, 2008, p. 17). The capacity to think, feel, and communicate is a uniquely human distinction; it is also the bedrock of society. Anything that delays access to language acquisition impedes all mental and emotional processes that depend on language to nurture their development.

Factors related to hearing loss that most greatly affect spoken language acquisition/development are the age at which the hearing loss or deafness is detected, the age at which consistent language stimulation becomes accessible, and the age at which use of amplification begins. Critical to a child's success is family support coupled with early intervention.

Early Detection Then and Now Needless to say, children who are deaf or have a hearing loss at birth and are not identified until later run a huge risk of having intervention services postponed until a determination of that nature can be made. Noted in a consensus statement by the National Institutes of Health

(1993, p. 3) was the fact that "The average diagnosis of hearing impairment remains constant at about 2½ years of age." The NIH goes on to say:

> Based on our knowledge of early childhood development, particularly that of language development, there is little question that a delay of this nature will have a monumental and most likely a lasting impact on communication and academic success, as well as social/emotional well-being. Research indicates [that] by far the most important factor that correlates with language achievement level for children with normal cognitive abilities is age of identification (Yoshinaga-Itano, C., Sedey, A., Coulter, D., & Mehl, A., 1998). This language advantage "was found across all test ages, communication modes, degrees of hearing loss, and socioeconomic status." (p. 1161)

As of February 2012, the National Center for Hearing Assessment and Management indicates that every state and territory in the United States has now established an Early Hearing Detection and Intervention (EHDI) program. The staff members of those programs are responsible for creating, operating, and continuously improving a system of services that ensure the following:

- Every child born with a permanent hearing loss is identified before 3 months of age and provided with timely and appropriate intervention services before 6 months of age.
- Every family of an infant with hearing loss receives culturally competent family support as desired.
- All newborns have a "medical home."
- Effective newborn hearing screening tracking and data management systems are linked with other relevant public health information systems.

Early Intervention and Family Support   With regard to the importance of early intervention, Moeller (2000) discovered that comprehensive early intervention is the critical variable. However, she also found that family involvement strongly contributes to vocabulary development and verbal reasoning skills. With respect to communication mode, Yoshinaga-Itano's review of the literature (2003) states the following:

> . . . early identification of hearing loss with early intervention was associated with better language development for all families regardless of method of communication. Families with early identification and early intervention who chose oral methods of communication, as well as those whose families chose communication with sign language, had children with significantly higher language quotients than children who were later-identified. No significant difference in the language quotients of the children by mode of communication selected by the families was found.

A home environment consistent with the provision of the necessary stimulation for a d/Deaf child requires parental acceptance, emotional responsiveness from the parent/s, accessible communication, a high level of parental involvement, and varied, consistent, and developmentally appropriate sensory stimulation.

Among the 5–10% of Deaf children born to Deaf parents, sign language acquisition is a nonissue and can serve as a basis for the development of spoken English should that be desired. They are welcomed into a home where ASL is most likely the primary mode of communication resulting in immediate and ongoing exposure to accessible language. There is an innate understanding of visual-spatial communication, knowledge of how to make eye contact with the child, and the ability to provide consistent language stimulation. As a result of early exposure to sign language, receptive and therefore expressive language tends to parallel the linguistic milestones and developmental expectations of a hearing child of hearing parents.

Amplification

Families who want their d/Deaf child to benefit from auditory input, including spoken language, environmental sounds, location of sound, difference between meaningful and non-meaningful sounds, and so on, should pursue the use of amplification. Deaf parents of Deaf children, whose identity resides with the Deaf community and culture, may feel that use of amplification is not desirable. Their native language and the language of the home is ASL, which is in no way dependent on auditory input for comprehension. A family's decision, when based on cultural and linguistic preferences regarding the use of amplification should be valued and recognized as valid.

However, if amplification is desired, critical to its effectiveness is the timeliness with which it is made available. Fitting a child with amplification and maintaining consistent use prior to the age of 6 months is essential, if there is a genuine expectation for the child to learn to attend to spoken language, discriminate meanings, and thereby approximate and finally gain competency in spoken English. Use of amplification precludes nothing in terms of communication options. In that regard there is no reason to delay its utilization and every reason to begin to stimulate the auditory pathways of the brain as early as possible.

Types of Hearing Technology Used with Infants

Three types of amplification can help develop auditory skills in children who have sensorineural hearing loss or deafness. These include digital hearing aids, cochlear implants, and FM systems. It is vital that auditory technology be coupled with appropriate auditory, speech, and language training if outcomes are to be optimal. Critical as well is utilization of the amplification system during all waking hours. FM systems are used to augment hearing aids and implants and are worn in specific situations to provide auditory access from a distance or in situations where background noise is an issue.

Early Development of Listening Skills   Auditory training is needed for a child to develop age-appropriate spoken communication skills. Such therapy trains the brain to listen and process information as it is received through the amplification device. When a child is young (birth–3 years), therapy typically focuses on teaching the parent how to provide auditory stimulation and a rich language environment. That changes to a child-centered approach as the child becomes a toddler.

Hearing Aids   Hearing aids can be fitted as soon as a hearing loss is identified, as early as 2 to 3 weeks of age. The earlier a child begins to utilize amplification, the greater the potential to demonstrate spoken language development commensurate with hearing peers. Behind-the-ear hearing aids are most often the choice for use with infants and can be fitted for any degree of hearing loss (mild, moderate, severe, or profound). Earmolds will need to be changed frequently (as the ear canal grows) in order to ensure a proper seal and thus transmit sound into the canal without complications of feedback noise.

Cochlear Implants   Children with severe to profound sensorineural hearing loss may be candidates for a cochlear implant (CI). However, current FDA regulations specify that infants younger than 12 months of age cannot be implanted. In those cases, children who are CI candidates wear hearing aids until the implant surgery can take place. Cochlear implants bypass damaged portions of the ear and directly stimulate the auditory nerve. Signals generated by the implant are transmitted through the auditory nerve to the brain, which identifies the signals as sounds. A cochlear implant is not the remedy many suppose it to be. The brain must be trained to interpret the signal it receives; without specific training, the implant itself is an expensive and intrusive device doomed to be less than successful. It is vital that parents who choose to utilize a CI understand that they need to make a huge commitment in terms of the time and effort necessary to achieve a desirable outcome.

Hope

Above all else, there cannot be cause for a loss of hope among parents—or professionals for that matter. Although the identification of a child's hearing loss may be traumatizing to parents, and information on deafness and hearing loss more than a little daunting, hope must remain a constant. There is, despite the stress of urgent decisions that have to be made, a vital need to believe that a positive outcome will be the likely result. The potential for silver linings . . . for good that can come from what may initially be viewed as devastating is something that should never be lost in the search for answers. Helen Keller (1957, p. 30) said, "Character cannot be developed in ease and quiet. Only through experiences of trial and suffering can the soul be strengthened, vision cleared, ambition inspired and success achieved"—an awe-inspiring concept that recognizes all that is within the realm of possibility. Language development, academic achievement, and healthy psycho-social emotional development can be the rule, not the exception, when early identification and intervention are coupled with strong family involvement and unwavering support.

The following poem was written by the parent of a baby boy born with Down syndrome. It has much to say about the philosophical shift that must occur in the hearts and minds of parents whose lives are graced with a child who was born differently from the one they had anticipated. I have shared the wisdom of this poem when asked to speak to families of recently identified deaf and hard of hearing children. It inspires and gives hope to those who may, at the onset, feel hopeless by presenting a metaphorical shift in perspective . . . one that encourages acceptance of what is, which in turn fosters the ability to explore what is possible.

Welcome to Holland

I am often asked how to describe the experience of raising a child with a disability—to try to help people who have not shared that unique experience to understand it, to imagine how it would feel. It's like this . . .

When you're going to have a baby, it's like planning a fabulous vacation trip—to Italy. You buy a bunch of guidebooks and make your wonderful plans: the Coliseum, Michelangelo's *David*, the gondolas in Venice. You may learn some handy phrases in Italian. It's all very exciting.

After months of eager anticipation, the day finally arrives. You pack your bags and off you go. Several hours later, the plane lands. The flight attendant comes and says, "Welcome to Holland."

"Holland?!" you say. "What do you mean, Holland? I signed up for Italy! I'm supposed to be in Italy. All my life I've dreamed of going to Italy."

But there's been a change in the flight plan. They've landed in Holland and there you must stay.

The important thing is that they haven't taken you to a horrible, disgusting, filthy place, full of pestilence, famine and disease. It's just a different place.

So you must go out and buy new guidebooks. And you must learn a whole new language. And you will meet a whole new group of people you would never have met.

It's just a different place. It's slower-paced than Italy, less flashy than Italy. But after you've been there for a while and you catch your breath, you look around, and you begin to notice that Holland has windmills, Holland has tulips; Holland even has Rembrandts.

But everyone you know is busy coming and going from Italy, and they're all bragging about what a wonderful time they had there. And for the rest of your life, you will say, "Yes, that's where I was supposed to go. That's what I had planned."

And the pain of that may never go away because the loss of that dream is a very significant loss.

But if you spend your life mourning the fact that you didn't get to Italy, you may never be free to enjoy the very special, the very lovely things about Holland.

—EMILY PEARL KINGSLEY, 1987

It is through the freeing power of acceptance and the adoption of an attitude of hopeful expectation that parents, with the un-wavering support of family, other families with deaf children, deaf adults, and professionals, can begin to move forward and adequately address the needs of deaf children and their families as a whole.

Chapter 4

Meet the Daniels Family

*Whenever I held my newborn baby in my arms, I used to think
that what I said and did to him could have an influence not only
on him but on all whom he met, not only for a day or a month
or a year, but for all eternity—a very challenging and exciting
thought for a mother.*

—ROSE KENNEDY, 1890–1995

It is difficult, if not impossible, to understand the complexities
faced by hearing parents of deaf children without first appre-
ciating some of the challenges d/Deaf individuals have confronted throughout history as well as controversies over issues of
communication and education that have created a decades-long
divide. The previous three chapters serve as a preface to the
story of the Daniels family and allow us to better appreciate their
dilemmas and enter into their reality.

No life experience compares with the anticipation of the
birth of a child in its ability to inspire hope for what will be. "I
spend my down time hoping to feel the baby move. Every kick,
punch, and swirl brings happiness to my heart. I love feeling
the movement. I love this child so much already. I can't wait to
meet her. I can't wait to hold her and kiss her fingers, cheeks,
and toes. And, yes, I can't wait to introduce her to this world."

Such were some of the thoughts and feelings that played
through Ginny's mind as she carried her daughter in her womb,
anticipating the birth and the changes it would bring to her life

and to that of her husband, Bob. Mingled with feelings of excitement and anticipation, however, intermittent and unvoiced "what if" questions surfaced from time to time. Considering the possibility of giving birth to a child with an exceptionality is most likely normal for most expectant mothers. For Ginny, who works as an activity therapy associate and nursing assistant with adults with developmental disabilities, such a possibility was one that could never be entirely dismissed, but it was not something that occupied a great deal of her attention.

Ginny and Bob grew up in the same neighborhood and attended the same schools. They became high school sweethearts and were married when Ginny was 23 and Bob, 25. After establishing themselves in their respective professions and purchasing a home, they began planning for the birth of a child. Ginny notes, "We were ready for a change in our lives and looked forward to the challenge of parenting." Upon learning of her pregnancy, Ginny began journaling in a "pregnancy diary." She documented normal neonatal development based on the results of a sonogram completed at 9½ weeks of gestation, adding, "Bob treats me like a queen." At 14 weeks Ginny recorded hearing the baby's heartbeat for the first time: "It was loud and strong." Kyler was born in the wee hours of December 8, 1988, the product of an unremarkable full-term pregnancy, labor, and delivery. Kyler and her parents were discharged from the hospital at 10 p.m. the following evening after enjoying a steak dinner provided by the hospital and visits from family and friends.

Reflecting on her demeanor at the time Ginny observes, "I had always been quiet and shy, Bob was much more outgoing. I knew I would have to become more assertive in my role as a mother. I started to come out of my shell a little bit when we attended childbirth classes. I wanted to know as much as possible about what I was embarking upon. Little did I realize that childbirth would be a 'breeze' compared to the unexpected roadblocks we would come up against while raising Kyler."

Their desire, as 30- and 32-year-old first-time parents, was to enjoy their daughter and delight in watching her grow, learn, and mature. Bob, a foreman with the city's property improvement program, went back to work almost immediately after Kyler and Ginny's homecoming. Ginny added two weeks to the standard six-week maternity leave at her place of employment in order to bond with her newborn and make sure caretakers were in place prior to her return to the workforce.

Ginny realistically reflects, "As I recall, life was good, but anytime you bring home a new baby there is stress . . . and [there are] questions. It was a totally different lifestyle." Among the stresses that had to be dealt with was the loss of Kyler's first two daycare providers in rapid succession after Ginny's return to work. Fortunately, Ginny was able to procure yet another daycare provider, one who was committed to caring for Kyler, following through on the feeding schedule Ginny provided, and providing the necessary stimulation for early childhood development.

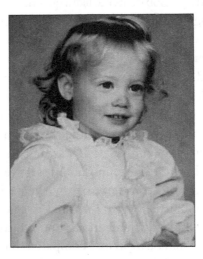

Kyler at 18 months.

According to Ginny, Kyler was an "easy" baby—one who slept and ate well and appeared to respond to the stimuli in her environment. During her first year of life Kyler was healthy, with the exception of a few sniffles and one ear infection, nothing unusual. She loved books from a very early age and seemed to have an uncanny awareness of all that was in her environment. She was visually attentive to movements and sounds . . . or was she?

At 11 months of age Kyler's childcare provider said, "I'm not so sure Kyler can hear." Ginny recalls, "That got me thinking. I was upset and took Kyler to see a friend and told her I didn't think Kyler could hear. We did some testing, banging pots behind her head, but there was no reaction. Her first birthday came shortly thereafter. When the party was over, Kyler was playing on the floor with balloons, and I popped one behind her head. She didn't move at all. I started thinking, she doesn't really respond to the dog. The dog barks like crazy. Nothing seemed to startle her."

Ginny took Kyler for her 12-month, well-baby checkup. "I mentioned a possible hearing loss to Kyler's pediatrician, and she said, 'Well, I would have never thought that to be the case, but you're around her more than I am, so let's have her tested.' Less than one month later, a local audiologist conducted an ABR [auditory brain-stem response] evaluation. He told us to keep her up all night long (which was very difficult) so that she would be tired in the morning for this test. They ended up sedating her anyway. I remember before we had the test done that morning, he clapped his hands behind her head, and Kyler turned her head. He said, 'Oh, I think she can hear some.' But we saw her hair move ever so slightly. The ABR test showed that the brain was not responding to sound."

Kyler's home state did not adopt legislation requiring universal newborn hearing screening until 1999, 11 years after her birth. Had universal neonatal screening been available at the time, the screening of Kyler's deafness would have occurred within hours of her birth. Visually attentive children often mask the fact that they cannot hear by visually alerting to movement, which is often accompanied by sound, thus creating the false impression that hearing is intact.

At 14 months of age Kyler was reevaluated at a world-renowned hospital near the nation's capital for a second opinion. The otolaryngologist's report reads as follows: "Kyler was never bothered by noise in sleep. The parents never saw her startled by loud noise. She points when she wants something. She appeared to be a visually very alert child. At no time did she respond to environmental sounds while being observed in the consultation room. There was no evidence of verbal language comprehension. Only vowelized vocalization was heard."

The doctor notes that, in a soundproof booth, when presented with low frequencies at their loudest volume, Kyler responded by turning toward the sound, an observation followed by this remark, "Sounds presented at that intensity are known to create vibratory sensations." Based on no response to sound in the middle and higher frequencies, despite presenting sounds at the audiometer's maximum-volume output, the conclusion was reached that Kyler's "consistent and reproducible conditioned oriented responses [or lack thereof] were indicative of a profound bilateral sensory neural hearing loss."

Ginny muses, "I remember the car ride home was very quiet. Bob and I both had a lot of thoughts going through our mind. I had asked the doctor what could have caused this. 'Is there anything I could have done?' I had a healthy pregnancy, everything was normal; I took care of myself before I was pregnant. He assured me that it was not my fault, that sometimes it just happens or that it [the deafness] could be genetic."

Bob recalls, "When we went to the hospital for the evaluation, I knew she was deaf . . . but I didn't know how deaf she was. I cried all the way home. I'm tearing up right now just thinking about it. It was good to get the results, but it was an emotional heartbreak. I'll be honest with you; I was pissed off that she was deaf ... not at her, not at Ginny, but at everybody else . . . God and the whole bunch of them. Acceptance was my biggest problem . . . and the questions. Why? Why my daughter? I know these things happen, but why to us? It was a bad place to be, but we made it through."

Ginny concludes the story of that day: "We had an elderly dog, Jetta; she was my 'baby' . . . my first baby. She couldn't hear and was nearly blind. She had begun to attempt to bite Kyler. That same day [after arriving home from the hospital], I took Jetta and had her put to sleep. It was one of the most difficult decisions of my life. But I just thought I couldn't deal with it; I feared the dog was going to bite Kyler. Kyler couldn't hear me say, 'No, don't touch.' That was a day of pure agony." Bob adds, "I'd always said when the dog needed to be put to sleep, I'd take her up in the woods and do it myself . . . but I couldn't. I said, 'With the emotional heartbreak I've had today, I can't do it.' Ginny said, 'You watch Kyler, and I'll take the dog to the vet.' When we got home, she took her dog that she'd had for years and had her put down [to eliminate any possibility that Kyler would be bitten]."

One thing about living in a small community is that everyone seems to know everyone else or, at the very least, to know someone who knows the person with whom you are not yet acquainted. So it was that Kyler's pediatrician knew me and called to request that I meet with Ginny and Kyler. Ginny's follow-up call resulted in what was to become a twenty-two-year odyssey for the three of us.

My husband and I had moved to his rural home county from a metropolitan area. I had grave misgivings about the move because it required that I leave my position as a speech therapist at the state school for deaf children. Living in a more isolated area, I feared, would result in the loss of signing skills, professional camaraderie, and the ability to access programs offering additional coursework in deaf education.

Shortly after our relocation, I was offered a position with my previous employer (the state school for deaf children) as a parent/infant educator. The arrangement would permit me to work in homes with families of recently identified deaf and hard of hearing preschool children in the westernmost region of our state. Such a position allowed me, for the majority of the week, to work within a sixty-mile radius of my home. One day a week I worked on campus, which gave me an opportunity to remain in close contact with my colleagues, maintain and continue to improve my signing skills, and keep benefiting from the school's aggressive staff-development agenda. After three years of itinerate teaching, I became pregnant. Following the delivery of our daughter I became a stay-at-home mom. Two years later our second daughter was born.

I continued my involvement with members of the Deaf community by interpreting worship services, as well as medical, social services, and legal appointments. This was prior to the days of the Americans with Disabilities Act. Such arrangements were both informal and gratuitous; thus I was able to arrive at a given location at a moment's notice with my daughters in tow to provide the needed interpreting service. I remember well arriving with a stack of books for my older daughter and manipulative toys for the younger one to keep them entertained while I signed and voiced the exchange between the deaf and hearing individuals.

I was named by gubernatorial appointment to the Board of Visitors, the governing board of the state school for deaf children. I had begun teaching sign language courses at a local community college and was also teaching courses and supervising graduate students who were completing practicum experiences through a graduate program at a liberal arts college.

At the time Ginny's pediatrician contacted me, my daughters were aged 5 and 7. Of importance at this juncture is the medical condition of our younger daughter, as I have no doubt that it factored into the way I responded to Ginny and Kyler. Our daughter had been diagnosed with juvenile rheumatoid arthritis. On certain days her joints were so stiff and swollen that she was unable to walk. At 5 years of age, only months after my initial meeting with Ginny and Kyler, our daughter had major eye surgery to relieve pressure that had built up in her eye, a complication of her particular type of arthritis. The surgery with its required week-long, daily, anesthesia-free injections administered directly into the eye prevented her from losing the eye itself, although her vision would thereafter remain permanently blurred. Throughout her early years she was shuttled to monthly appointments with eye specialists, rheumatologists, and our local family practitioner.

My husband and I were faced with making treatment decisions often based on conflicting information. Treatment outcomes were frequently positive, but others had negative effects. Possible long-term consequences of her condition ranged from total remission to the fusing of all major joints and dependence on a wheelchair for mobility as well as possible loss of vision in what was now her "good eye."

The obvious parallel with Ginny and Bob's situation is the factor of the unknown. When it comes to the physical or medical conditions of one's child, not knowing the impact the condition will have is the greatest source of concern—and fear. Fear, if not resolved or translated into action, can paralyze. It becomes the nightmarish "monster under the bed," rendering parents incapable of moving forward.

Initial Interaction with Ginny and Kyler

It was against this personal backdrop that Ginny and I became acquainted. Our relationship from the beginning was uncomplicated, enhanced by what seemed to be a bond between mothers of daughters, mothers dealing with unanticipated circumstances. We discovered that we shared the same birthday, as well as a yearning for spiritual well-being, acquaintance with a realm beyond ourselves, a realm that would lend a sense of purpose to our current realities. I daresay that Ginny confided in me no more than I confided in her. Our relationship evolved into one of mutual trust.

No longer employed as a teacher, I was released from my role as parent/infant educator, espouser of the current philosophy of how best to teach young deaf children. From the beginning of our relationship, Ginny and I seemed to be able to create a space where total honesty was practiced. I did not feel as if my training in the field of deaf education was null or that I no longer had an opinion about how to teach deaf children. I did feel, however, that all possibilities, all options must be explored (no stone left unturned) until Ginny arrived at a place where she felt confident about Kyler's potential for success. I was no longer entrenched in a philosophical paradigm that did not allow for reaching outside the box to consider other options. I was a professional, yes, but also a mother of daughters for whom I wished the best in all areas of their lives. I desired no less for Ginny and Kyler.

Without a full-time work schedule to impede my activities and with my daughters in school, I was able to spend significant amounts of time with Ginny and Kyler. My daughters were thrilled to have a young companion during their days at home, an audience of one who would laugh hysterically at their antics and give them her undivided attention. In time, Kyler imitated their actions, which were accompanied by perfectly mimicked facial expressions and mannerisms. Each animation was completed with the skill of a well-trained actress.

In addition to grabbing moments for "our girls" to be together, I visited Ginny and Kyler twice weekly for the following two years. During that time, I modeled signed communication during noonday meals, bath time, while sorting laundry, playing outside and inside—taking advantage of the language-rich environment that is home.

Kyler was 13 months of age at our first meeting (1989). She was cherubic in looks. Her blond hair lay like spun gold in soft natural ringlets framing her porcelain-skinned face, delicately calling attention to her long-lashed, baby-blue eyes, which, chameleon-like, changed to azure, green, or Caribbean blue depending on the color of her clothing. Although shy by nature, upon arriving at a level of comfort, Kyler would act out all of her observations, imitating real-life characters as well as those she had seen in books and on television. She was innovative in choosing items from her environment that would allow her to "become" the character of the moment. Many times I expected Kyler to jump into the page of a book, joining the characters in their realm, much like Jane and Michael Banks had leapt into Bert's sidewalk-chalk artistry accompanied by their nanny, Mary Poppins. Kyler's imaginative play and interactive signed and gestured communication were accompanied by lips opening and closing in silent imitation of observed movements of articulators, movements that carried no sound to her deaf ears, the imitation of which did not disrupt the stillness or disturb her revelry.

While spending a great deal of time labeling all that was in Kyler's environment, Ginny and I also made use of photographs, giving "sign names" to each family member and all those with whom Kyler came into regular contact. I encouraged Ginny to keep a written account of Kyler's signed vocabulary, which she diligently maintained. The vocabulary log began on March 5, 1990, with a listing of 18 single signs. In May of that year Ginny noted that Kyler had begun vocalizing more and had signed her first sentence: "Eat cheese, please." Ginny documents in the log, "She really seems to associate saying 'Mum, Mum' with 'Mommy.' She says it a lot when she wants out of her crib." At 28 months Kyler signed her first article spontaneously in the following sentence: "The dog eat." In December of 1991 Ginny wrote the following notation: "Hundreds of words signed from 4/91–12/91 . . . can't keep up." Kyler had begun asking questions and responding to all manner of questions asked of her. A final entry recorded just prior to Kyler's third birthday reads as follows, "The girl is in bed with the bear."

A general rule of thumb is that at 1 year of age children tend to communicate in single-word utterances, at the age of 2, two-word utterances, and at the age of 3, three-word utterances. After that, utterances tend to expand in length and complexity, no longer corresponding to chronological age. As demonstrated by Kyler's recorded sentence, she was communicating in multiple-sign sentences by the age of 3. The sentence quoted earlier consisted of eight signs, an amazing accomplishment for a child not exposed to accessible language stimulation until the age of 14 months.

Kyler at 2½ signing, "There duck fly." She is pointing and signing DUCK at the same time, adding FLY in the second frame.

Kyler on horseback at 2½ — love at first sight.

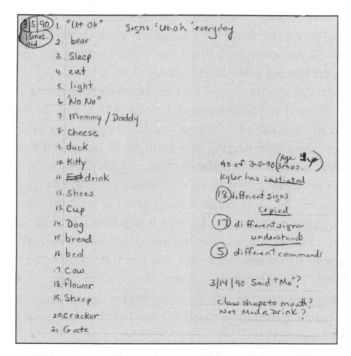

A page from the vocabulary diary Ginny kept of Kyler's sign acquisition.

Audiological Intervention

At 13 months Kyler was seen by an audiologist at a university speech and hearing clinic, a close personal friend of mine; a professional with multiple years of experience evaluating preschool-aged deaf and hard of hearing children and fitting them with amplification. Kyler's first audiology appointment followed auditory brain-stem response evaluations and initiated the process of fitting Kyler with hearing aids. Ginny summarizes the outcome of audiological intervention: "She was fitted with hearing aids; her diagnosis was profound deafness bilaterally. We tried behind-the-ear aids. We tried a body aid and an auditory trainer. We tried some kind of vibrotactile device, too. But she didn't respond to anything; it didn't really seem to matter." Ginny recalls the result of subsequent visits to the university clinic: "It just confirmed that Kyler wasn't getting any benefit from the hearing aids. Ann, you were there."

Indeed, I was there, and I remember well Kyler being fitted with binaural amplification and the expectation that she would begin making use of whatever residual hearing was available to her. Decreased hearing was thought to be exacerbated by frequent retention of middle-ear fluid and middle-ear infections; antibiotic treatment was recommended at the first sign of congestion. As Kyler became more familiar with the expectations regarding follow-up hearing evaluations the audiologist noted, "Her responses became more consistent and her response to sound more dramatic." When Kyler was 2 years old, a Phonic Ear FM system was introduced to maximize speech input by lessening the influence of ambient/background noise, thus reducing the signal-to-noise ratio and thereby providing a clearer speech signal.

Kyler's response to amplification in her everyday environment did not reflect the findings in the testing booth. I remember the slow dawning that, despite the consistent use of hearing aids, Kyler was not orienting to sound, attending to speech production, or attempting to reproduce sounds or words. I accompanied Ginny and Kyler to their final audiological appointment at the university, joining Kyler in the soundproof booth. I wore a protective headset to prevent damage to my own hearing during the evaluation. I distracted Kyler with a ball of masking tape (sticky side out) while the audiologist introduced sounds into the booth. The purpose of the distraction was to minimize the possibility of a false response on Kyler's part. Various frequencies at ever-increasing volumes were presented; Kyler's eyes remained on the ball of tape as she rotated it inquisitively in her hands. It was only when the volume was sufficient to create vibrations that Kyler's gaze left the ball and searched for the cause.

The determination was made that Kyler was not receiving sufficient benefit from her hearing aids and that it might be wise to consider other options. By this time, Kyler was 2 years, 5 months of age, necessitating a quick decision if cochlear implant surgery was to be an option while Kyler was still young enough to obtain maximum benefit. The audiologist noted the following in his report: "Information regarding cochlear implant programs will be provided to Kyler's family." True to his word, he provided Kyler's parents with information about cochlear implants and hospital sites currently performing cochlear implant procedures.

Early Educational Endeavors

The most important period of life is not the age of university studies, but the first one, the period from birth to the age of six.
—MARIA MONTESSORI

Soon after my initial meeting with Ginny and Kyler, I contacted my former colleagues in the Family Education / Early Intervention

Program at the state school for deaf children. In September 1990 they began providing weekly services to Kyler, who was at that time 14 months of age, and her family. Their goal was to make available to parents knowledge about deafness and to equip hearing parents with signing skills sufficient to provide consistent language stimulation and allow for reciprocal signed communication. This was accomplished by modeling language-rich interactions with Kyler.

Additionally, Kyler began receiving services through the county's Infants and Toddlers Program in March of 1990. These services included weekly speech and language stimulation provided by either a speech and language pathologist or the school system's teacher of deaf children. The case manager noted the following: "Loving, supportive, very secure environment. Strong family support network with numerous members of the family enrolled in a sign language course at the community college. The family is accepting of Kyler's disability, has contacted appropriate personnel for services, and is eager to learn about Kyler's needs."

Assessment data at 28 months indicated the following:

Cognitive skills are appropriate for her age. She adapts to form board reversals, identifies colors, knows the use of objects and understands size differences. Her language skills are at the 28 to 36 month level with some skills at a higher level. She signs in phrases, relates experiences from the past, knows several colors, knows prepositions and size differences and is beginning to express emotions through signs, but has not begun to imitate vocalizations. She imitates play activity, role plays and can participate in simple games. Kyler's self-help skills are at the 30 month level.

So it was that Kyler, during her preschool years, despite living in a rural area, benefited from an array of services that included parent/infant education, sign language interaction/modeling, speech and language therapy, and audiological intervention.

The only thing missing was the benefit from amplification. This would preclude the possibility of acquiring spoken language.

Philosophical Shifts in Deaf Education and Their Bearing on Kyler

Our state school for deaf children had in 1967 adopted what was called the "Total Communication" philosophy. Total Communication fueled the hope of finding middle ground in the age-old dispute between oralism and manualism, restoring a lost regard for sign language, and elevating reading levels for high school graduates (which at the time hovered at a third-grade equivalence). These anticipated results were cause for great excitement among parents, administrators, and teaching staff alike. While the first two goals were partially realized, reading levels for those graduating from schools espousing the new philosophy remained virtually unchanged, a result that was a devastating blow to those who had maintained high hopes that the glass ceiling for literacy achievements for deaf children would finally be shattered (see Johnson, Liddell, & Erting, 1989).

During my involvement with Kyler and her family, I taught a number of graduate courses (1983–1998), all of which were related to language and speech acquisition in d/Deaf and hard of hearing children. One of the texts selected for use by the Deaf Education Department of the college was Stephen Quigley and Peter Paul's *Language and Deafness* (1984). The authors noted that exceptions to deaf adults' poor reading abilities were found among those who enjoyed infant and early childhood learning experiences, early schema development, cognitive and linguistic development, making inferences, and engaging in figurative language and who also demonstrated the ability to use speech coding and recoding for processing text. In other words, findings were very positive for children who at an early age had experience with learning models that supported the development of language acquisition, thinking skills, vocabulary development and a link between signed and spoken words that would later translate to better reading skills. Speech recoding was found to be important for hearing readers, not so much for access to word meaning as for temporary storage of words in the working memory, which allows for the comprehension of clauses and sentences. "This is one aspect of memory where deaf persons have been found consistently to have shorter spans than hearing persons" (ibid., p. 148). Although such abilities can be acquired in the absence of hearing, it is not typically the case.

Even though Kyler had the advantages of early childhood learning experiences, excellent cognitive abilities, and linguistic development, her ability to develop speech coding and recoding skills without the benefit of residual hearing was, for me, a huge concern. Although some successful deaf readers have no auditory input, they are the exceptions to the rule. Research at the time revealed generally poor reading levels among deaf high school graduates, which affected their academic skills across the board. Inferior reading levels among high school students persisted in large part due to weaknesses in English language competence as well as the inability to speech recode, a skill requiring temporal-sequential memory and one that is dramatically influenced by auditory input—or lack thereof. I expressed my concerns to Ginny as she considered how to respond to Kyler's inability to benefit from more traditional types of auditory intervention.

Total Communication Didn't Live Up to Expectations

Documentation of the failure of Total Communication to alleviate poor reading skills and weak academic achievement was extensive in the late 1980s and 1990s (Quigley & Paul, 1984; Johnson, Liddell, & Erting, 1989; Grosjean, 1992; Strong & Prinz,

1997; Erting, 1992; Johnson, 1994; Nover, Christensen, & Cheng, 1998; Svartholm, 1993, 1994).

As a result, beginning in 1990 with the Indiana School for the Deaf and continuing today, numerous programs and schools for deaf children began to embrace a bilingual-bicultural approach to teaching deaf children. The BiBi approach asserts that American Sign Language should be the first language of d/Deaf children in the United States and that English should be taught as a second language. The ultimate goal is proficiency in ASL and written English, as well as the attainment of social ease in both the Deaf and the hearing culture.

Ginny's choice to use sign language with Kyler was an easy one, in large part because of the additional delay that most likely would have occurred if an oral-only philosophy had been embraced, particularly in light of Kyler's lack of response to auditory stimuli. In addition, Kyler's rapid gains in vocabulary and connected language, as a result of exposure to sign language, was an exhilarating confirmation that using signs with Kyler was of great benefit. Although studies examining the Total Communication methodology had shown it to be less promising than hoped, there was as yet no track record on the use of a bilingual-bicultural approach with deaf children. BiBi remained in its infancy with no research on its efficacy. As a result, Ginny chose to use spoken English simultaneously supported with signs with Kyler.

Accessing Auditory Input: Is a Cochlear Implant the Answer?

Prior to Kyler's third birthday, she was evaluated at a medical center at Ginny's request to determine whether she would be a candidate for an implant. Criteria for children for whom a cochlear implant was being considered included a profound sensorineural hearing loss in both ears, little or no benefit from hearing aids, no medical contraindications, high motivation with appropriate expectations (by child and parents), and placement in an educational program that emphasized the development of auditory skills after the implant had been activated. Kyler and her parents met the criteria, and the decision was made for her to receive an implant. "We didn't just jump to [the decision to] have cochlear implant surgery right away. There was a year of making sure that Kyler wasn't getting anything from her hearing aids."

Upon Ginny's request, the implant team provided her with a list of parents willing to speak with her about their decision to have their child receive a CI. Ginny first created a written list of questions and concerns and then contacted each of the families, posed her questions, and recorded their answers in a journal. It is clear that her deliberation to have Kyler undergo cochlear implant surgery was weighed with a heavy heart. She wrote the following: "Problem I am having is: How did you justify to yourself the risk you are placing on your child for a surgery which was not medically necessary? How did you explain what was going to happen to your child? Did you say 'You are going to have an operation to help you hear'?"

At the time, Ginny and I talked at length about the pros and cons of the surgery. Although not wanting to influence the final decision, I must say that I was not unhappy when Ginny opted for the surgery. She recalls that it was a difficult decision for many reasons but especially because Bob did not wholly support surgical intervention. Ginny feared that, if the surgery were unsuccessful in any way, she would be to blame. Bob held the view that a cochlear implant was not a necessary surgery:

> If she'd needed a transplant, or if surgery had been a matter of life and death, it would have been easy to allow them to operate. But this was a gray area . . . a matter of "quality of life." Anything can go wrong when you go under the knife. To think of them messing around with her brain, cutting her

head open—was too much. She was my baby girl, she was born deaf, and I'd love her no matter what . . . whether she had a cochlear implant or not.

In the end Bob went along with Ginny's decision: "Ginny was much more affirmative about the CI. Ginny is very level headed; she's very intelligent. If I want the right answer, she has it; so I went with her on this decision. I trusted her judgment because she's never let me down in the past. I'm the one who makes bad decisions . . . surgery for Kyler was a decision I didn't want to make."

The doctors made it clear to Ginny and Bob that the surgery should not be considered a "quick fix." Ginny recalls the doctors explaining that "It will be a forever, never-ending process of learning how to use the implant and [continued follow-up] testing, and you have to be committed to it. I was warned that Kyler wasn't going to put it [the receiver] on and go with it. With any surgery there are risks." Ginny justifies the surgical procedure and numerous follow-up appointments this way:

> After trying amplification with no benefit and knowing she was a bright child, I wanted to offer Kyler options to help her get through life and communicate the best. She's not from a family that's deaf; we are all hearing. I thought the cochlear implant would be the best option to help her communicate with both deaf and hearing individuals. I talked to other parents who had opted [for their children] to have the surgery, and I asked a lot of questions. It seemed like a cochlear implant was worth the chance. I watched some videos on children who had received cochlear implants. I understood the surgical procedure . . . the implant would be [permanently] in her head. If she didn't like it, or if she didn't want to use it later in life, she didn't have to wear it. She would be able to choose to use the cochlear implant or not when she was old enough to make that decision. The surgery was stressful because it was not a surgery that was a medical necessity. It was a choice, a life-changing choice."

Bob now agrees, "I look back at it now and say it was a godsend."

Ginny recalls the time constraint involved, "There was a time factor as well. If we were going to get it [cochlear implant surgery] done, we needed to get it rolling because the earlier, the better. I talked to somebody who mentioned an adolescent who'd had it [cochlear implant surgery] done, and he decided he just wasn't wearing it . . . there was too much peer pressure. He'd grown up without it, and when you try to do something like that to an adolescent during the rebellious years, it is likely to fail."

Thus, after a day of blood work and preliminary testing, Kyler received a cochlear implant on March 31, 1992. According to Ginny's recollection, Kyler was the 41st child to receive an implant at this particular out-of-state university hospital. Implants were just beginning to be performed on adults with late onset deafness at an in-state hospital of greater renown. However, at that time the in-state hospital had not performed a single cochlear implant surgery on a child. As a result, Ginny opted to go with the medical team that had the most experience despite the fact that more than $5,000 of the medical costs would have to be

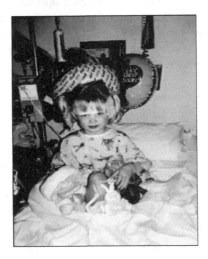

Kyler following cochlear implant surgery.

paid out of pocket. This additional financial burden was due to the medical insurance provider's unwillingness to fully cover a procedure performed in an out-of-state facility.

Ginny was given a pamphlet developed by the company that created the Nucleus 22-Channel Cochlear Implant System (the system that Kyler would use). The pamphlet details the following differences between hearing aids and cochlear implants:

> Hearing aids and other assistive listening devices simply amplify sound (i.e., make it louder). However, sounds provided by even the most powerful and effective hearing aids may not offer much useful benefit to those with profound bilateral hearing loss. A cochlear implant, on the other hand, is designed to provide useful sound information by directly stimulating the surviving auditory nerve fibers in the inner ear. (1989)

Approximately six weeks after the surgery, Kyler was to have the electrodes activated at a level that she could comfortably tolerate. Input would be regulated during successive visits until amplification provide a "sense of sound" at a volume similar to that of an individual with normal hearing.

Kyler insisted that her friends needed their ears bandaged as well (2½ weeks after surgery).

Opposing Views and an Independent Decision

State School for the Deaf Staff Opposed to the Implant

Ginny recalls an experience just one day prior to Kyler's surgery:

> Some of the faculty members at the state school for the deaf were not very supportive of cochlear implants. We were leaving the following day to have Kyler's surgery when someone from the school faculty called me at work and said, "We really wish you would reconsider this surgery . . . that you would let her make her own decision when she's of age. You could possibly be making it more difficult for her to be part of the Deaf community and be accepted." I thought, "She's not part of the Deaf community; she's part of our community." The phone call just added more stress to an already difficult situation.

The state school for deaf children would not officially adopt a bilingual-bicultural model of education until August of 1993, one year and 10 months after Kyler's implant surgery. However, the waves of change had begun prior to the school board's vote to make it official, as is evidenced by the phone call Ginny received at work about her decision to pursue the surgical option for her daughter.

At the time of Kyler's implant surgery (1991) neuroscience had yet to establish the fact that when the auditory pathways are not stimulated early in life, the brain is less able to make use of aural information as time passes. The situation is comparable to that of individuals born with congenital cataracts that prevent them from obtaining visual experience in early childhood. As mentioned in chapter 3, they grow up to be functionally blind even after the cataracts are successfully removed (e.g., Sacks, 1993). A more thorough explanation of the impact of postponing cochlear implant surgery in terms of the brain's ability to make use of the new information it receives is given in a September 10, 2009, blog by a parent identified as

K. L., who posted the following on the ASL–Cochlear Implant website, http://aslci.blogspot.com/ (accessed 09/24/09):

> Many Deaf children's advocates recommend waiting to implant until the child is old enough to decide for him or herself if they want to get an implant. If all else was equal, I would be right there with them. The problem is that for the implant to be successful, the brain needs auditory input during the critical first three years. If hearing aids work for the child, great, waiting is good. However, for the profoundly deaf infant, hearing aids are rarely adequate in providing the needed auditory information across all the pitch ranges necessary to acquire verbal language. Therefore, waiting for the child to decide is the same as choosing not to implant at all. Because the chances are good that if you implant the 10 year old child who has had little to no previous auditory input, the implant won't work for them. It is not that the implant can't give them sound, it is that the child's brain is no longer able to adequately process that sound into meaningful information. So parents actually have no choice about letting their child decide. If they choose to wait and let their child decide, they ARE deciding. They are choosing not to implant. To implant or not to implant is, by default, a decision the parents WILL make, whether or not they even recognize that they are the ones doing the deciding. If you truly believe that this is a decision the child should make when they get older, how do you address the reality that by the time they get old enough to decide, they are too old to make good use of the sound the implant will give them?

Neuroscientists have accumulated compelling evidence to suggest that children with shorter durations of deafness prior to their implants fare better than children with long durations of deafness (e.g., Wilson & Dorman, 2008; Blamey et al., 1996; Summerfield & Marshall, 1995; Gantz et al., 1993). Speculation is that the result of sensory deprivation for long periods, which adversely affects connections between and among neurons in the central auditory system (Shepherd & Hardie, 2001), may allow other sensory inputs to encroach on cortical areas normally devoted to auditory processing (i.e., cross-modal plasticity; see Balvelier & Neville, 2002). In other words, the brains of children become less "plastic" or adaptable to new inputs beyond their third or fourth birthdays, which explains why deaf children implanted before the age of 3 generally have better outcomes than those implanted later (e.g., Lee et al., 2001; Sharma et al., 2002; Dorman & Wilson, 2004).

Medical Staff Opposed to Continued Use of Sign Language following the Implant

Ginny recalls that "At the medical college [where Kyler's surgery was performed], the audiologist and physician felt that continued use of sign language would hinder Kyler's ability to process the sound she would be getting from the cochlear implant. They felt that she might not try to make the best use of the implant because she already had signs to rely on for communication." This attitude among many in the medical community (and some audiologists) is not something that has only recently emerged as the result of the dawn of cochlear implants but rather is a myth that has been perpetuated since the earliest use of amplification. Despite evidence that the use of signs promotes early language acquisition, which is the foundation for the development of spoken language, for some implant teams, the legend continues.

The medical team would have much preferred that Ginny stop signing with Kyler. She explained:

> I felt that would be devastating for Kyler . . . to just take away sign language. I prayed that sign language would enhance the use of her implant, not detract from it, and that it would help clarify the sounds she was hearing. If she could pair signs with sounds and words, she could make sense with the implant rather than signs being something that would distract her from the so called sound; (it's not really sound; it's electrical

stimulation). I can't even imagine how you would associate electrical impulses with words and understand if you didn't have something to connect it to. That was my thought. It was our hope that sign language would enhance the use of her cochlear implant, and it did indeed, as far as I'm concerned.

Being drawn into a philosophical debate during this anxious time of decision making introduced additional tension into Ginny's life. It created an unfortunate burden during a time that was already fraught with the weight of the importance of the decision at hand and with the pressure of being sure that it was the correct decision for Kyler.

Ginny asserted that "I guess they [the medical staff] thought the cochlear implant was powerful enough for kids just to depend on speech. I guess that's why they developed that technology . . . to make deaf kids function like hearing kids."

A Combined Approach Was Maintained

Ginny persevered in her conviction that sign language would augment Kyler's language and speech acquisition despite being cautioned by both sides of potential pitfalls resulting from a sign-supported speech protocol. If the implantation were successful, there would be no need for sign language. At least that was the theory espoused by the medical team. Concerns expressed by the professionals at the school for deaf children, on the other hand, dealt with their fear that Kyler would become disconnected from the Deaf community, a community that Ginny—and eventually Kyler—felt was not theirs. Regarding sign language and its benefit Kyler observes, "It really helped me connect words to their meaning; it was my main way of learning. Without signs, I don't know that I would have been able to keep up with my same-age peers in school or have been able to go on to college."

Kyler's Initial Response to the Cochlear Implant

The initial records from the medical center document Kyler's audiometric results before and after the implant along with scores from a battery of formal and informal vocabulary, language, and speech evaluations. They contain no mention of Kyler's initial response to sound either when the electrodes were first activated six weeks after the surgery or later, at the six-month follow-up appointment. The audiologist's report from her 12-month cochlear implant follow-up appointment also included no information on her response to the programming and mapping of the implant. Of the 22 channels in the implant, only 21 could be successfully implanted due to the size of Kyler's cochlea. After Kyler's CI was activated and programmed, the determination was made that two of the electrodes were considered to be "hot" and had to be turned off in a follow-up visit. The result was that Kyler has functioned with the use of 19 channels rather than the original 22. Ginny recalls no explanation of what was meant by "hot electrodes." Information about Kyler's two "hot electrodes" and having to terminate their use is absent from her medical and audiological reports.

My recollection of the time immediately after the activation of the electrodes is one of horror. I recall Kyler arriving home from the activation appointment with a broken blood vessel in her face as a result of screaming and crying during the mapping process. She was so sensitive to sound that moving a piece of paper startled her. Introduction to the world of sound was an unpleasant experience, to say the least. I called the clinic and, after describing Kyler's hypersensitive reaction to speech and environmental sounds, asked whether the intensity could be adjusted. Steps were taken to "remap" Kyler's implant, the result of which was a much better ability to tolerate auditory input. We have no way of knowing whether Kyler's hypersensitivity to the mapping process was a result of the "hot electrodes" and whether, as a consequence, the pain was sufficient to cause her to scream with such intensity as to break a blood vessel in her face. Because Kyler could not adequately communicate the cause of her anguish, her parents, surgeon, and audiologist were in the dark as to what she felt or how to determine what trauma may have resulted from that particular incident. Ginny speculates that it is the memory of that episode that has plagued Kyler to the point that she becomes tearful each time the CI is remapped. Kyler's emotional response is one that continues to this day.

I remember feeling an overwhelming sense of responsibility and guilt with regard to the immediate results, concluding that never again could I support the decision for a deaf child to receive a cochlear implant. I recalled reading ancient tales of boric acid being poured into the ears of deaf children in an effort to "open" their ears and restore hearing. The practice produced horrific burns to and scars on their ears and face but did not, as one can imagine, enable them to hear. I pondered the possibility that cochlear implants might be the 21st century's parallel to such attempted cures of the past.

Thankfully, those thoughts and the accompanying guilt were a brief affliction. Kyler's extreme sensitivity to sound was temporary, and afterward she benefited mightily from the implant. Ginny concurs: "There was a period of time when we weren't so sure that Kyler was going to benefit from it [the cochlear implant]. She was uncomfortable with it at first. That was, I think, the only time I recall thinking, 'maybe this wasn't a good idea.' But that was short lived."

Acceptance

As a parent with no previous exposure to or knowledge of deaf individuals, Ginny ponders her ability to accept Kyler's deafness:

> I've often wondered if my career as a teacher and caregiver for individuals with disabilities for the past 30 years helped

me accept this challenge. I feel that God chose me to be Kyler's mom because I could deal with her deafness. I've felt blessed to have been chosen to have this experience. My belief is that God is in control, no matter what happens, and He will get us through. He is the guiding Force. I'm sure my faith has made a difference [in my acceptance]. When a decision had to be made, we put it in God's hands, and everything seemed to work out. We prayed, asking for answers to the obstacles we were facing. You invited us to come to church, and that experience was something that really opened me up to my faith.

Ginny adds after a pause: "I won't say there weren't struggles in trying to figure things out. I don't want to sound like everything has been wonderful and that I didn't worry, that I gave everything to God and it worked out . . . or that this [life with a deaf child] has always been rosy—because it has not."

At my invitation Ginny and Kyler began attending a church where I had interpreted for deaf congregants for 10 or more years. Although Ginny was a member of another congregation, I extended an invitation because I thought exposure to an interpreted service could assist both mother and daughter in their sign language acquisition. They would also be in contact with d/Deaf adults with whom conversational sign language could flourish and also be among a community whose members had long been supportive of d/Deaf congregants. From that time until Kyler's graduation from high school, I served as the interpreter for worship services and Sunday school sessions and occasionally served as teacher for Kyler and her Sunday school peers.

Reflecting on the impact Kyler had on her life during those early years, Ginny muses: "Just having her, just the fact that I had a baby for one thing. As far as her deafness goes, I felt like every step of the way Kyler encouraged me. I can recall when she was about 5 or 6 years old; I said to her, just randomly,

'How did you become so special?' And she said, 'God made me that way.' "

Kyler attributes her self-confidence and sense of self-worth mainly to her mother and her faith. Kyler reminisces: "She [Mom] was sure things would work out. I guess I got that positive attitude from her . . . faith probably had a lot to do with it. Before I would go to bed, she would say a prayer with me. I've seen prayer create miracles, and the power of prayer . . . that it really does work. Faith has made me a stronger person and [helped me] make better decisions in life. I always liked my Sunday school teachers. I liked going to Sunday school, of course. It was fun to go to school on the weekend to learn the Bible stories. They [the teachers] made a way to make it fun to learn about the Bible. And also I always liked to sign along to the songs. That was my favorite part!"

When asked about her sense of self-worth, Kyler responds, "He [God] decided to make me special, and He made sure that He gave me to parents that would accept me and not give me up for adoption like some parents would . . . or get rid of me. I think He created each one of us special, and He decided to make me deaf to bring a change on Mom's life, a positive, necessary [change] . . . not negative." Ginny laughingly concurs, "Drastic [change]!"

During her elementary school years, Kyler and her mother worked with the children's choir at what had now become their church, teaching the children signs for choral musical selections. Kyler remembers that she became so interested in music that she and neighborhood friends wrote songs together. "I wrote one song called, 'Are you ready for heaven?' I thought it was inspiring to write little songs . . . I might be embarrassed about that now. I have songbooks we created. We recorded our songs on a voice recorder. I hope I burned that tape . . . a deaf person singing—I don't think so." Kyler giggles at the remembrance of it.

A Series of Miracles or Happy Coincidences

There seems to be a string of happy circumstances that have followed Kyler throughout her life. Ginny recalls, "Everything has fallen into place. Our pediatrician knew you. You knew the audiologist and teachers at the school for the deaf. Kyler's preschool teacher [at a local nursery school] just happened to be a certified teacher of the deaf. She wasn't using her talents or skills at the time, and when Kyler came along she could do that. Also, you were a big connection when we needed an educator for the deaf [for the public school system]."

I contacted a teaching colleague from a nearby state who willingly joined the local public school system, initiating what became the first and only satellite program affiliated with the state school for deaf children. Deafness is a "low-incidence disability," meaning that its occurrence will be infrequent among any age group in a given population. However, as noted in a local newspaper article in recognition of the five-year anniversary of the program, "There was an unusual cluster of children who were very close in age and had significant hearing loss or deafness. The program [was] developed because parents of deaf and hard-of-hearing children did not want to send their children away to school. The parents were concerned about being placed in a situation where their children would leave Sunday at 2 p.m. to go to the state school for the deaf and not return until Friday evening" (Martirano, 1997).

The article continued as follows: "A committee emerged that helped arrange the program's administrative and academic goals, as well as the needs for its kindergarten and preschool students. An agreement between the county school system and the state school for the deaf in cooperation with parents whose children are involved in the program is completed every year. It includes an adjacent county which pays tuition [for its students]" (Martirano, 1997).

Funding for the satellite program's teaching position came from the governor's budget (a line item from the budget of the school for deaf children) with the local school budget funding employment of the two teaching assistants. The program served six children from prekindergarten through second grade, was the only one of its kind in the state, and was on occasion used as a model at national conferences on deafness. Kyler's parents were quoted in the article as saying, "The program is perfect for Kyler. There has never been a concept that this dedicated teaching team can't get across to Kyler." The team consisted of a certified educator of deaf children and two instructional assistants with signing skills. The affiliation among the schools continued until Kyler graduated from elementary school, after which time the state school for deaf children and the county remained on very good terms with the school providing consulting services on an as-needed basis throughout Kyler's graduation from high school.

One of the most important of those "happy coincidences" for Kyler, who has a penchant as well a great gift for art, is that she was the beneficiary of a cadre of excellent art teachers who supported and encouraged her talent throughout her public school education and into her college years. As a result, she has been the recipient of numerous art awards and has through the years had her work displayed locally, nationally, and internationally.

Kyler began drawing at a young age, an interest that both Bob and Ginny promoted. Bob, however, takes credit for Kyler's artistic gene pool. The drawing below was completed by Kyler at the age of 2 years and was drawn upside down. I found Kyler's drawing so fascinating that I purchased and read the text *Drawing on the Right Side of the Brain*. One of the primary techniques that the author, Betty Edwards, uses is to place an item or a picture upside down and have her students reproduce the model from that orientation. She insists that the endeavor will result in a switch to reliance on the right side of the brain, unleashing creative abilities among those linear thinkers who find their artistic abilities subjugated by the left hemisphere of the brain. Elliot Eisner (2002), professor emeritus of art and education at the Stanford University School of Education, asserts, "The right hemisphere provides the location for much [*sic*] of the visualization processes; it is the seat of metaphoric and poetic thought, and it is where structure-seeking forms of intellectual activity have their home"(p. 99).

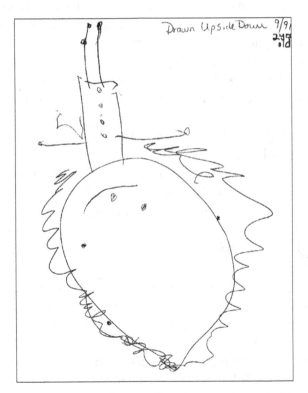

Kyler drew this figure when she was 2 years old.

Chapter 5

School Choice

Education is not the filling of a pail, but the lighting of a fire.
—WILLIAM BUTLER YEATS

Elementary School

As mentioned previously, beginning shortly after being identified as having a profound hearing loss and continuing for the next three years, Kyler received weekly visits from teachers through the public school system as well as the school for deaf children. At the age of 4, she attended a full-day program at a local elementary school. The only documented note of conflict occurred during Kyler's first year as a full-time student and was recorded in her individualized education program (IEP). The speech therapist speaks in support of a recommendation made by the cochlear implant team, which was that Kyler be "integrated into a regular [education] program. Emphasis needs to 'de-emphasize' sign and begin [development] of a [spoken] language base." The speech therapist added that "Kyler has had in-depth training in sign and is ready for more."

The deaf educator, on the other hand, expressed the feeling that Kyler did "not have the internal language to use an interpreter in kindergarten" and recommended that Kyler not attend kindergarten at all that year. A compromise was reached: Kyler would participate in a regular preschool program two afternoons, a regular kindergarten two afternoons, and a self-contained classroom for deaf children 4 half days weekly.

During kindergarten, first, and second grades, Kyler interacted with a normal hearing student population during lunch, recess, art, and physical education classes. During third grade, she was intermittently integrated with her hearing peers for science and social studies. Throughout the fourth and fifth grades Kyler was fully included for all nonacademic subjects as well as science and social studies. I served as her interpreter and provided academic support services for the subjects for which Kyler was mainstreamed. Additionally, Kyler received speech therapy four to five times weekly for the duration of her elementary schooling.

As a result of the collaborative effort between the two county school systems and the school for deaf children, the only school placement Ginny considered was Kyler's home school in the county public school system. Ginny elaborates on school choice: "When we chose to have the cochlear implant, the school for the deaf was not an advocate of that, and Kyler was doing well with it. I wouldn't want to send her to a school where the teaching theory was to use ASL, with no voice. It wouldn't work with Kyler's cochlear implant . . . there would be no reason for her to have an implant."

Kyler shares the following reflection on school choice:

The thought of going to a school for the deaf never crossed my mind. I was comfortable here. It is home; my family is here. When I went to the school for the deaf [to visit], I talked to other kids that said they missed their family. But the school was also their home. I did not see the school as my home, and I didn't like the thought of living away from home at such a young age and riding the bus back and forth. I had friends here, I was already established here, and I thought I was getting a good education. I was getting good grades, so why not [continue]? It never crossed my mind to change [schools] and go with the other deaf kids. It would have been a dramatic change in my life; you know how I don't like change. I'd have had to leave my comfort zone.

Ginny adds to Kyler's thoughts, "As long as Kyler was thriving here and being educated and was content, [I was content]. As she got older, if she would have said, 'I don't want to be in the public school; I want to be with other deaf children,' I would have honored her wishes."

The county school system continued to maintain an excellent working relationship with the state school for deaf children and often requested the school's advice on specific matters. It also sought ongoing student evaluations to assess the continued efficacy of the county's program. This positive association continued despite the fact that not a single student from the county opted to attend the state residential school for deaf students.

Kyler reflects on her elementary school experience:

> In elementary school, they [the deaf education staff] did kind of isolate all the deaf kids. There were eight of us at the time in our classroom. But they made sure that we branched out into hearing classes, starting out with gym and art, with other kids. As I got older, they put me in more hearing classes with other kids with interpreters. I don't think I ever really felt isolated because we went off to the playground with the other kids and ate lunch with them; we socialized that way. They encouraged it; they didn't keep us in the room all the time. I think that helped.

Kyler asks her mother, "Were you concerned about peers, the other kids . . . how they would treat me?" Ginny's response reflects her intermittent anxiety: "I think I always have been concerned . . . I still think about this. I was concerned that you would feel left out, or . . . they [the children] wouldn't play with you because there was a communication gap. But, when I look at these pictures [of Kyler's childhood years], and I talk to other people that we socialized with, it seemed that she just 'rolled with the flow' and was accepted." In an attempt to reassure her mother Kyler adds, "Growing up, I never really felt isolated, not that I remember. Always, I had friends in the neighborhood. I grew up with the same hearing friends [from] elementary through high school . . . everyone just accepted me."

Ginny actively participated in all school meetings and events. It is important to note that she never missed a single IEP meeting throughout Kyler's prekindergarten, kindergarten, elementary, middle, and high school years. The signature page attached to the annual IEP forms requires that all participants sign their name to indicate agreement with the proposed education plan as well as to document attendance. As Bob candidly admits, "Ginny was the glue."

Middle School

When Kyler completed the fifth grade, she, along with three deaf classmates, entered middle school. The teaching staff who had begun teaching Kyler as a 4-year-old accompanied the students to the designated middle school. The four students, their teacher (who was a certified deaf educator), and two instructional assistants occupied a self-contained classroom, with the students coming and going as was indicated by their IEPs.

Kyler's sixth-, seventh-, and eighth-grade IEP reads as follows: "Kyler's hearing loss impacts her ability to benefit from regular education without the support of a deaf education classroom or interpreting with remediation for Reading, Mathematics, Written Language, and Spelling." Kyler's education plan called for following the "regular education curriculum for Science and Geography with adaptations and accommodations as needed." With the exception of the sixth grade, during her middle-school experience, Kyler was "included" for the creative arts classes, which consisted of physical education, technology education, home economics, and art. Kyler and her classmates were exempt from taking the otherwise required music class.

In response to class setting options, when given the choice to accept or reject a "general education class" placement, Kyler's teacher checked "No." Her teacher gives the following reason for rejecting that option: "Kyler's needs require a more intense placement." Kyler did, however, participate with "nondisabled peers" for meals, assemblies, field trips, athletics, recess, clubs, and regular transportation. It is important to note that the deaf educator established all of Kyler's educational goals and objectives as well as placement recommendations and that the educator's recommendations were accepted by the IEP team at the time of the meetings. Kyler continued to receive 30 minutes of individual speech therapy three times weekly throughout her middle school years. Both amazing and critical to Kyler's spoken-language development is the fact that she was able to retain the same speech therapist from the age of 4 through middle school. I served as the speech therapist for students in the program briefly while the regular therapist recovered from a broken foot. Otherwise, she was the constant in that realm.

Kyler reminisces about her elementary and middle-school experience: "I had the same teacher and the same teacher assistants for 10 years, until high school. That was scary because we were close to them, comfortable with them." Throughout those 10 years, Kyler and her deaf classmates got together (during the school year and summer vacation) with their teacher and instructional assistants. They celebrated students' birthdays, holidays, and special school events. At their teacher's home, they had pool parties and barbecues; they even had tea parties, where the students learned the proper etiquette for an English high tea. Theirs was a liaison that was not confined to the classroom but extended into relationships with one another's families, outside the bricks and mortar known as school. As a result, this small group of students and their teaching staff became a very close-knit community.

Kyler and I also maintained a bond that extended outside the boundaries of school and church. She accompanied me to pick corn at my parents' farm in the mountains to our west and to the Southern States Feed store to purchase 200 bluegill fish, which we released into the farm pond. Kyler and I staged a Halloween party at my house, decorating it for the gathering. Our purpose was to get the middle- and elementary-school deaf students together. After sharing the same classroom for three to four years, the two age groups lost contact with each other when the older group matriculated to middle school. Arts and craft activities were set up for the children based on age and interest, with Kyler being on the creative end of the undertaking. My daughters came home from college to join the festivities.

The relationship Kyler and I shared was one that crossed and connected the boundaries of mentor, friend, teacher, speech therapist, school, church, and home. These border crossings were conducted with a sense of ease and comfort perhaps because the connections evolved over time and perhaps because life in a small community is often comprised of various individuals who become relevant to one another in multiple venues.

Regarding having the same teacher and instructional assistants for such a lengthy period Kyler surmises:

> It was beneficial because we were comfortable. They knew what made us "touchy" [have hurt feelings] and what subjects we were weak in. So they emphasized those subjects and kept working with us over and over again. They knew what NOT to do to make us cry . . . [Kyler laughs] because we were sensitive. But when it was time for us to separate from them, I think there was more anxiety than there would be with kids that have had a different teacher every year.

Kyler observes that there were more positives than negatives regarding her educational programming: "I don't like change; I like to be comfortable in my situation. They knew what they were doing;

my teacher was certified in deaf education and everything. They got familiar with us and knew [our] weaknesses and strengths."

Kyler recalls not being "mainstreamed" for math until the eighth grade: "Mr. Lafferty was really my first certified math teacher." As to whether that posed a problem for Kyler regarding her math skills, she responds:

> You see, we only had one certified deaf education teacher, and then we had two assistants that were not certified teachers. They knew sign language. They were personally good in math, but they were not certified to teach it. I felt more confident with them rather than mainstream, but I'm glad I stayed with it [math in the mainstream class]. English was strong because the deaf educator was certified for English; she had a separate degree for English. She really worked with me a lot. We read stories, poetry, and we went over every topic of English and grammar rules . . . we really worked on that a lot.

As a seventh-grade student, Kyler wrote the following rough draft in her school journal:

> In the summer of 2001, my mom and I read in the newspaper about a Multicultural Art Contest downtown. My mom said that I should join the art contest. I said sure, it will be fun to join the art contest. So I joined. I got started on my painting. We went to the store and got a heavy backboard, a special watercolor sketch pad. I went on painting my picture. It was an Indian riding on the horse through the river and there was a waterfall, and woods around the river. The Indian was hunting and spotted a turkey up in a tree. He was pointing his bow and arrow at the turkey. It was called "Hunting on Horseback." I took it downtown to hang up in a big glass window with the other pictures. Later, a man called and told me to come downtown for an award ceremony. Also he said that I won First Place! So, I went down and got my award. My parents were very proud of me. We hung up the picture and the award plague [*sic*]. It took hard time drawing that and a long time too. I am very proud of me!

Kyler's award-winning entry in the Multicultural Art Contest.

Kyler recalls going into homeroom classes with the teacher of the deaf students and her deaf classmates to teach sign language to teachers and other students:

> They [the classroom teachers and hearing peers] were interested. That's why most of my peers growing up knew sign language. Ann, you also taught after school sign language courses in elementary school. . . . Most of them [fellow students] just picked up enough [signs] to talk to me, and some just were interested in being able to know another language . . . just interested for their own enjoyment. But, especially my best friends, the ones I hung out with regularly, they could interpret for me pretty much. I had one childhood friend who could REALLY interpret for me.

At the age of 10½, as part of a class journal-writing assignment, Kyler wrote the following about herself:

Athletic, Funny, Smart, Artistic

Daughter of Ginny and Bob

Lover of . . . Horses, amusement parks, sports!

Who feels . . . Proud when achieves something, Happy when having fun with friends or family, Sad when a good friend moves away.

Who needs . . . to keep room clean every day, put thinking cap on before school every day, go to bed at 10:00 for a good night sleep for school.

Who gives . . . hugs and kisses to family, gifts to family or friends for birthdays, funny or cool drawings to friends

Who fears . . . snakes, spiders, bees

Who would like to . . . be a vet, work with horses, or an artist

One would assume that the words preceding the dots were provided by the teacher and that the students filled in the blanks with ideas of their own choosing. Kyler's self-description suggests that she was a loving and conscientious child who knew herself well and had a positive sense of self.

Kyler has always been an animal lover and was indulged by her parents in that regard:

> I always had multiple small critters throughout the years . . . always had something in an aquarium. I loved my fish and still have them. I had names for all of them. I remember devoting my spare time to doing weekly / monthly water changes growing up. I had a special pair of Goldfish that I won during a game at the annual fall festival in WV, which was a treasured family memory. We visited and stayed with my Dad's grandmother, Nanny. They [the goldfish] lived a good 10 years. I remember having such pride for being able to maintain them that long.
>
> My favorite fish now are the ones I rescued. I am not kidding . . . I rescued probably around 100 goldfish from being flushed

at the Country Club when I was a banquet server there while I was going to the community college. They [the fish] were featured in wedding centerpieces. I found homes for all of them, and kept 10 for myself. I have one special large fish right now . . . who is also a rescue, a yellow bellied mud catfish. Daddy saved him from his fishing pond in WV by his cabin, about 6 years ago. At the time he was barely an inch long, and would have been eaten by other fish within seconds. He swam into a bait bucket by the boat. His name is Mr. Whiskers. He is now thriving, and almost a foot long.

Other critters I had in aquariums over the years were hermit crabs, a tropical green tree frog, and Anole lizards. Of course, I had names for them all. Hermit crabs especially have a decent lifespan. I have classic childhood memories of all of them. Robin the frog and Speedy the lizard were a special pair. I took such pride in them. I took them to elementary school for show and tell. Robin leaped out of my hand into the crowd of children watching and was found hanging off the eyeglasses of a girl whose name coincidentally was Robin. She was not amused . . . she began screaming and waving her arms around which sent Robin the frog flying across the classroom onto the metal ledge of a chalkboard. Speedy, the lizard was known for running off. He went missing in the house for a month or so. You kind of loose [sic] hope after awhile . . . until one day I was feeding live crickets to the others in the aquarium and dropped one onto the floor. There leaping out from under the bed skirt was a skinny Speedy . . . who gulped the cricket whole!

I also had one hermit crab in particular that I lost while playing doll house. I'll never forget daddy coming into my room while I was getting ready for school telling me that the crab was still alive. It was just chugging across the carpet downstairs while dad was reading the newspaper on the couch. That crab had been missing for a good 4 months. I guess it lived off bugs. The odd thing was it went missing from my bedroom . . . I guess it crawled clear across the house then rolled down the steps!

I had two rats. Fiona was my first one. I remember begging
my parents for her as a Christmas present after seeing her in
the pet store. I will never forget how creative they were at sur-
prising me on Christmas morning. Daddy said he was thirsty
and handed me his cup so I went around the corner to the
Roaring Springs water dispenser, and there sat the aquarium
with Fiona in it. I just remember how thrilled and happy I was.
She was one of the best gifts ever!

With regard to activities unrelated to school, Kyler played on
a church league basketball team with her mom serving as her
interpreter. Kyler was also a dancer for 10 years. She speaks about
how, as a deaf person with a cochlear implant, she was able to
function in her dance classes: "you have to depend on [the] music,
and the vibrations . . . the beat. Most deaf people feel [music]
through their bare feet or [they] put their hands on the stereo for
the beat. I didn't really have to do that [because of the CI]."

An independent psychologist who was herself Deaf was
hired by the school system to evaluate the middle-school deaf

Christmas pictures of Kyler and her pets. The photo on the left
was taken at age 12 and the one on the right at age 16 (note the
rats perched on Kyler's left shoulder).

students. She noted that Kyler's drawings on the Bender Gestalt were "neat and very well drawn; a clear indication of her artistic ability is evident. Her perceptual motor skills are excellent. No emotional indicators are evident; this is seen as a protocol of a well-adjusted child." When asked to draw designs that were shown and then withdrawn, Kyler "was able to reproduce 7 of the 9 designs perfectly. Excellent visual memory is evident."

During this time Kyler's speech reception threshold, or the volume at which she could respond to spoken language, was determined to be at 35 decibels, just slightly louder than the norm of 0 to 25 decibels for individuals with normal hearing. Her auditory discrimination skills, as evaluated by the medical center implant team, were continuing to improve. Speech perception data indicated that she understood 100% of the "common phrases" that were presented in the testing situation, as well as 87% of the phonemes (sounds in isolation), indicating that Kyler's implant was enabling her to do all that had been hoped for.

High School

In a statement sent to the high school Kyler would be attending as a ninth-grade student, with regard to "Present Levels of Performance" her teacher noted: "Kyler has successfully passed all of the Functional Tests," adding that, during eighth grade, Kyler had been "included" in a regular education classroom for the following subjects: science, U.S. history, math, and the creative arts courses. The teacher's report continues as follows:

> Kyler has maintained all As in both her inclusion classes and her classes in the deaf program classroom. Much of Kyler's success is a result of programming which has allowed time for remediation and ongoing clarification of all concepts and vocabulary occurring in these inclusion classes as well as Kyler's own conscientiousness and ability to study, memorize material, organize herself and work hard every day. Kyler's

independent reading level is at the fifth-grade level. However, more difficult material can be attacked with shared reading, guidance, and a slower, more careful pace which allows for explanation and in-depth study. Kyler has had difficulty with math throughout her school years, and while she has had success in the eighth-grade math class, her true understanding of some of the material is at best questionable. Some of her more basic math skills are "shaky" as well. Kyler has good study skills, and her ability to attack textbook information, written tests, worksheets and additional written material has improved a great deal over the last three years. Kyler has outstanding artistic abilities and can produce beautiful, creative finished products when given a "project" that involves the use of artwork.

Kyler's teacher of deaf students often said that she did not plan to accompany her students to high school and chose her students' exodus from middle school to high school as her appointed time of departure. Coincidently, Kyler entered high school in the fall of 2003, the year that the federal law known as No Child Left Behind (NCLB) took effect. In addition to numerous other requirements, this law made it compulsory for all students to have teachers who were considered to be "highly qualified." Teachers were deemed "highly qualified" if they had certification at the elementary level or certification in a given subject area (e.g., math, science, English) for middle and high school.

The unique impact this had on students receiving special education services is that they could no longer be taught, as had previously been the case, by a teacher whose certification was in the field of special education or, in this case, in deaf education. As a result, Kyler's program of study changed completely. She and her deaf peers would now be "fully included," meaning that they would be taking all of their courses with their hearing peers from teachers who knew nothing about deafness or how deaf students might best learn. The local board of education provided an interpreter and a note taker for each class.

I became the service coordinator for the deaf students in the county. My responsibilities included coordinating interpreting and note-taking services, as well as conducting a study hall class, during which time I tutored and provided supplemental instruction to Kyler and the other deaf high-school and elementary students. Because Kyler's former teacher was concerned that English in "an included environment" could be a potential area of difficulty, I interpreted for that class. The interpreting assignment provided me with firsthand knowledge of the topics being covered in class, and I was thus better equipped to provide supplemental information during our study period. Kyler continued receiving weekly speech therapy during her high-school years, meeting with her therapist before the school day started in order to avoid missing academic classes.

The county had no choice but to hire interpreters through an interpreting agency in a neighboring county because there was no local pool of interpreters from which to draw. I spent many mornings meeting with the interpreters to discuss both the code of ethics established by the Registry of Interpreters for the Deaf for educational interpreters and the importance of being familiar with the subject matter being covered in the classrooms. The school system continually dealt with interpreters' absences; in one instance an interpreter missed approximately 25% of her afternoon assignments. An additional burden for the students was coping with interpreters who had varying degrees of competence, as well as significant variations in sign vocabulary as compared to the signs to which the students were accustomed. Of the pool of interpreters utilized, only one had certification. Unfortunately, this is a fairly common problem, especially in more rural areas. The school system also faced difficulty in attracting and retaining a program director, in part due to its rural locale.

Kyler addresses the difficulties:

They [the school system] had a hard time finding a [permanent] director of the whole deaf education program. They hired somebody from California and moved someone here from Louisiana who was willing to work, but it just didn't work out. So sometimes we were without a director. Sometimes it was just interpreters, and students, and tutors. But I think the frustrations were mostly with the interpreters, because you had to learn their signs. Their signs were different. We were willing to learn their type of signing . . . and got comfortable with them over time.

Extracurricular activities posed additional problems because it was necessary to find interpreters who were willing and able to remain after the end of the school day. Kyler nudges her mother, "You were the interpreter pretty much." Kyler recalls, "There were not interpreters available to stay after school for my practices. I think there were more problems with the after-school programs than with the in-school programs. It was hard when one deaf student had cheerleading and I had basketball, track, cross-country, and then another student had color guard. So you know they didn't really have enough interpreters who were willing to stay after school and do all that."

Ginny remembers frequently interpreting for Kyler in those situations—"in the locker room and on the bench" when Kyler played basketball, an awkward situation both recall ending after the county was eventually able to procure additional interpreting staff.

Kyler continued to earn excellent grades throughout high school despite changes in program directors and the frustration of coping with interpreters who possessed varying skill levels. As a ninth-grade student, Kyler was nominated by her English teacher and selected by the school faculty to be featured among fellow female students who exemplified "Women Inspiring Hope and Possibility." The selected students were featured in a booklet that highlighted a female from each high school whose contributions to her school, church, and/or community were commendable. Examples given in the booklet of Kyler's community involvement were participation in Relay for Life,

Math-a-thon, the American Heart Association's "Jump Rope for Life," sign language instruction with a children's choir at church, and helping with young children during vacation Bible school.

Kyler was invited to join the National Honor Society during her sophomore year; she had the distinction of being the first deaf student in the county to be recognized with such an honor. In addition, Kyler was the recipient of athletic, achievement, attendance, art, and citizenship awards throughout her high school years.

Socially, Kyler admits to having only a few close friends, one of whom was a female classmate who was also deaf. However, she was always found on the dance floor with a date at high school dances and was a regular at school athletic events. Kyler laughingly refers to her high school years as a time of "high drama" among her female friends and classmates.

Kyler's art abilities during her high school years earned honors locally as well as in state and national competitions (see pages 106–107 for a few of her favorite pieces).

A butterfly-tiger Adirondack chair painted for a charity fundraiser auction.

A section of a mural painted on a child's bedroom wall.

Autumn leaves.

Chapter 6

College and Beyond

College Coursework, Life, and the Future

As mentioned in the introduction, Kyler graduated in the spring of 2012 from a local university, where she received a bachelor of fine arts degree in art and design with a minor in art history. Prior to that, she attended and graduated magna cum laude with an associate of arts and sciences degree in art and design.

Kyler considered herself to have been a "nontraditional college student" because "I was a deaf student attending a 'hearing' college. I required the use of an interpreter in each class and note takers. I couldn't be looking down taking notes the whole time. I would miss everything the interpreter was signing. The interpreter was next to the teacher. I listened to what the teacher said, and if I missed something, I looked over to my interpreter." The lag time between the instructor's speech and its transmission through the air was sufficient that Kyler could look back and forth as needed in order to access information that was not clear auditorily. Which did she rely on more, the interpreter or the teacher? "It probably evened out; I probably depended on both [the instructor and the interpreter] equally. I liked hearing the teacher as well as watching the interpreter." Without an interpreter, Kyler says she might be able to understand the lecture if she "sat in the front row and asked a lot of questions." "It would depend on whether they [the instructors] have an accent, or if it is a male or female . . . it just depends on a lot of factors."

Someone might ask, "If your CI is so successful, why would you need an interpreter?" Kyler responds that the use of an interpreter allows her to be sure of not missing anything important. "Everyone has a different tone of voice. Some people are easier to hear and understand than others. I don't understand males as well as females because their voice is deeper. Also, I'm more of a visual learner; I learn better from the added visual component of an interpreter."

Kyler elaborates:

However, when I raise my hand in class, I'd rather talk for myself; I never had the interpreter talk for me . . . unless the teacher didn't understand. Then the interpreter would repeat what I said. But that didn't happen very often. I know a lot of people have the interpreter be their voice, but I never used that option. If I was in front of the class to give a speech, the interpreter always sat in the audience; I talked for myself. By the time in the semester that presentations had to be given, all my classmates knew me, knew that I was deaf and that I may mispronounce some words . . . so they knew what to expect. In the past I've printed out my whole speech and given a copy to everyone in class so they could read along if they wanted to. I am "independent" when it comes to speaking for myself, but still "dependent" on an interpreter [for receiving information in a classroom setting].

Often in a large classroom, it is difficult to hear other students . . . especially if they speak quietly and are speaking from behind me. So an interpreter is definitely necessary. Sometimes the interpreter or teacher will have to say [to the students], "Please speak up a little bit."

A benefit that Kyler enjoyed was the fact that her interpreter at both the community college and the university was one of the teaching assistants who had worked with her throughout elementary and middle school. By both accounts theirs was a comfortable association resulting from their close, longtime relationship in the public school setting.

With regard to getting the university to provide the necessary accommodations, Kyler acknowledges that it was sometimes challenging. She admits to acquiring self-advocacy skills during her final two years of college by necessity. The breaking point, according to Kyler, was during her final semester, when she was making plans to attend a university-sponsored cultural-exchange course in China. The university was convinced that she could get a sign language interpreter after arriving in China. "I'm like, Chinese Sign Language vs. American Sign Language . . . they are not the same. They [the university advisors] couldn't understand that. I had to go to the ADA [Americans with Disabilities] person on campus. I'd never met her until my last semester of college. She turned us [Kyler and her interpreter] down. So we went to the president of the university." The president made the determination that Kyler's interpreter would be permitted to travel with her to China at the university's expense.

When asked whether she considered herself to be a "typical" college student, Kyler's response was as follows:

> No. I can say I wasn't your average college student. I focused more on studies and my art work than anything. . . and working. I worked part-time for an area resort as a server and began working at a veterinary hospital as well during my final semester. So I was going from school to work and then home. I didn't really have a social life in between. I think most kids party during college. I never really liked that scene. When they were going to parties off campus . . . I never really did that. Kids in my class would say, "We went to a party last night; it got busted," and all that stuff. I was at work . . . that was my choice.

With a giggle Kyler says,

> I was kind of a nerd. . . . I'm not saying everyone partied, but often it's the main point of their being in college . . . and making friends. Also, students at the university weren't as social as students at the community college. It was really weird. They

isolated themselves a lot . . . headphones were a big thing. They didn't like to have a conversation; they preferred being in their own little world listening to their music. At the community college there were more students sitting outside talking. Sometimes at the university in my Art Studio class (it was relaxed, and you could talk while you were doing artwork) I'd be talking, and then I'd realize that they [other students] had their headphones on. I'd be like . . . "Well, okay, guess I'm talking to myself." I'm pretty talkative for a deaf person.

Kyler and Ginny agree that majoring in art worked to Kyler's benefit. In addition to the fact that Kyler had considerable talent, most art classes had a hands-on component. Studio classes, Kyler explains, have a limited class size so that teachers can offer more personal instruction and assistance with individual students working on art projects. It was a scenario that resulted in a one-on-one communication environment, which was advantageous for Kyler.

Kyler admits to being unsure of exactly "where she wants to go" in the field of art. After taking her first graphic design course she was unsure how she felt about using computer-assisted software and "not having control" as compared to using pencil and paper. As a result, graphic design is not her favorite art medium:

I don't see myself working in a school. I think I'm too shy to teach in front of kids. Also, I would have to work with deaf kids, not hearing kids because I wouldn't be able to communicate perfectly with them. I'd hate the fact that I'd have to grade papers. I see myself more as a freelance artist working out of my home . . . as a business. You know, make custom artwork for people out of my home, enjoy the comfort of home, and being my own boss. I don't like the thought of working under someone, like in a big company . . . sitting in a cubicle behind a desk, or something.

Regarding the continued use of her cochlear implant Kyler says, "I will always use my CI because it allows me to live a more normal life. I get upgrades every two years. My insurance pays for that." Ginny quickly interjects that the insurance pays—but not without a lot of haggling.

Kyler adds:

> I notice with every technology change to the cochlear implant that I'm hearing more environmental sounds, sounds I've never heard before with the "Freedom" CI that I have now. The other day I heard a woodpecker, and I didn't know what it was. I was walking my dog with Mom, and I said, "What was that?" Mom said, "That was a woodpecker; haven't you ever heard that before?" I said, "No."

Addressing the possibility of adding a second implant, something that is becoming increasingly popular, Kyler says, "Probably not. I like the way I'm functioning. But if it got to the point that I didn't think I was grasping enough or hearing enough information . . . maybe. We'll see . . . if in married life, I couldn't understand, or with my kids . . . but technology might be changed enough by then. They [cochlear implant manufacturers] are beginning to make them more powerful . . . so [we'll see].

Kyler returns to the university clinic for annual reprogramming. "They go in and 'clean-up' the map, remap it, then take me in the 'sound room' and test me to see how I'm functioning. Based on the results, they will look at the audiogram and see if I'm doing better or not and make necessary changes. The 'Freedom' has four programs. I still don't fully understand it, but one setting is for concerts. It blocks out the background noise and focuses on the singer. There are different settings; there's a setting for 'one-on-one' conversation, and there is a 'basic' setting." Regarding her appointments to remap her CI, Kyler admits, "I lose my sense of comfort . . . I don't like change in general. It gives me a headache every time they do it [reprogram the CI]; I don't know why. Maybe it's the constant beeping. The last time I didn't cry, but most of the time I cry. I get real emotional; I don't like change. Then after a week, I'm comfortable with the new map. I just always give myself a hard time in the beginning. The process is not physically painful; it's just annoying."

Our community is one with only a handful of d/Deaf adults, most of whom are old enough to be Kyler's grandparents. Because of the small numbers of d/Deaf people and the disparity in their ages, Kyler has had few chances to mingle with other d/Deaf individuals of similar age. Such opportunities are more often enjoyed by d/Deaf persons living in more urban areas. Kyler occasionally sees a former high school classmate who is Deaf. She is a current graduate student living elsewhere. "We hang out when she comes into town to visit family." Kyler notes their differences:

> My friend's college had a number of d/Deaf students enrolled and offered a major in Deaf Studies. After starting college, she adopted ASL as her main mode of communication. She has a Deaf boyfriend and is very much involved in the Deaf community. I learn new signs from her when we are together. She always makes fun of the way I sign (I sign more like a hearing person). Once I visited her where she now lives; we went to a basketball game at a school for the Deaf. My eyes got tired from watching so much signing; I'm just not used to it. I am more verbally expressive than the typical deaf person. I remember when my friend went off to college and took ASL classes; she was amazed at how different ASL is. She met people who use ASL. I never really had the opportunity to socialize with truly Deaf/ASL people. I feel overwhelmed because they sign so fast.

Kyler and her friend are wonderful examples of autonomy and self-definition. Both are successful young deaf women with similar educational backgrounds (they were educated in the same classroom grades pre-K–8). They shared the same teaching staff and speech therapist, and both are cochlear implant recipients. Yet one has chosen to remain in her home community, where she identifies more with a hearing population in terms of communication and associations, while the other has chosen to leave the area, adopt ASL, and embrace the Deaf community. These young women illustrate a small slice of the diversity seen among d/Deaf individuals. Exhilarating is the fact that each has had opportunities to explore, evolve, yet they have chosen divergent paths in how they communicate with and relate to others.

With regard to how the CI has helped her function socially, Kyler says, "It has helped me have a broader social life. I've always had hearing boyfriends and hearing friends. We hang out, go to concerts, football games . . . the regular things. I have more hearing peers than deaf peers. I always arrange for an interpreter when we go to concerts. Sometimes when we are in a concert or a professional sports setting, I wish everyone could sign; we wouldn't have to lean in to try to have a conversation."

Kyler relates her love of music:

> I go to concerts every summer. This is probably rare for a deaf person to say . . . but I do . . . I enjoy music. In order to understand the words in a song, I look up the lyrics on the Internet and follow along with the songs over and over again, and I kind of memorize [the words]. I can sing along or read along. After hearing it so many times, I don't need the lyrics because I know them by heart. I can just follow along and know what the singer is saying. I like to listen to the radio when I'm driving by myself.

What about barriers? Ginny says, "Kyler doesn't pick up the phone and make her own appointments. She will call me and ask me to make an appointment. I know deaf people do that kind of thing themselves. She had a job interview, and the person was going to call Kyler. I had to get on the phone and set it up as a conference call to make sure Kyler understood everything."

Kyler elaborates:

> I do rely on my mom for doctor's appointments and that kind of thing. I don't understand people whose voice I'm not

familiar with. I'm independent in certain ways, but in that way, I'm not. I just always feel so insecure about the phone. You can't see the person's lips or their face. Even using the video relay system, you don't see the person you called; you only see the interpreter. So it's awkward signing to a person you don't know on a video screen. Some people love that; they use it every day. But deaf to deaf, or deaf to hearing, it still doesn't promote that relationship because you're looking at an interpreter. You have to have patience to use the TTY relay system because you have to pause while you're waiting for the other person to respond. It's very time consuming. Skype and Face Time are possibilities, too, but businesses currently don't have Skype or Face Time set up for people to use to communicate with them.

Kyler's father notes that as a result of the CI, Kyler's "enunciation is great. She put in a lot of time . . . a lot of summers and had a lot of help. I think through all the experiences she has had, she can adjust better in the hearing world. Kyler can communicate with anyone. Today, she doesn't have a problem as far as communication . . . even in her work. I'm so proud of her, I really am. She is still growing and evolving, and it still amazes me. She has excelled; she's still excelling, and I hope she never stops."

Self-Perception: "deaf" or "Deaf"

It [deafness] is just part of me, not who I am. I see deafness as a special gift.

—KYLER

James Woodward (1982) was the first to capitalize "Deaf" in reference to the cultural practices of a group within a group. Woodward utilized "deaf" written in lowercase letters to refer to the condition of deafness and to the larger group of individuals with hearing loss who may or may not have formed a connection to a cultural, linguistic, minority model of deafness.

Since that time the distinction has become a conventional practice in writings pertaining to d/Deaf individuals.

When asked how Ginny and Kyler view Kyler's identity, Ginny responds, "I would say 'deaf' with a small *d* because, without her cochlear implant, she can't hear anything." Kyler quickly agrees. Ginny continues, "When she's wearing her implant, she functions more like a hard of hearing person. In many circumstances, she can understand what's being said, and her speech is intelligible, but she has limits. If there's too much noise, background noise, the tone of someone's voice, the speed that someone's speaking . . . then she needs the interpreter to clarify. So I think of her as hard of hearing. Without her implant . . . she is deaf."

Kyler concurs:

I strongly feel [I am deaf] with a little *d* because I don't really use sign language as my main communication any more even though I learned sign language first, before [spoken] English. Now that I'm older, I talk more than I sign. It [deafness] is just part of me, not who I am. I agree with what Mom said, when my cochlear implant is off, I can't hear; I'm deaf.

I'd rather sign with d/Deaf people and with interpreters (to make sure I'm getting everything). It [speech reception] just depends on the situation. If I don't have my CI, if it's not working, or [if the environment is] dark or loud, [then] I wish that hearing people could sign to me, too. In normal situations, I don't need hearing people to sign to me. They just need to talk, not real slow, just at a normal pace, clear . . . and not mumble.

When I meet deaf people who wear hearing aids or none at all, they ask me, "Do you have a cochlear implant?" They state their opinions about it. But I say, "I'm glad that my parents made this decision for me. I like my life the way it is." I fit in better with my peers in this town, in school, and on the job.

Kyler explains her habits regarding communicating with another d/Deaf person: "I never turn off my voice, and they [deaf individuals] always get shocked that I use my voice and move my lips. That's the way I was raised . . . to talk and sign at the same time." Kyler quotes her longtime teacher, "Always sign with your voice." She adds, "Unless we have to be quiet somewhere, I always use my voice with deaf people."

When asked whether, given the opportunity to have normal hearing, she would "go for it," Kyler responds, "I don't know; that's kind of a hard question. I probably wouldn't because I like the way I am. There must be a reason God made me deaf. I just see it [deafness] as a special gift. I wouldn't want to be 'hearing' because I like some of my advantages, like if something is too loud, I can turn it [the cochlear implant] off." Kyler laughs about enjoying a slow transition in the mornings: "I don't like to put it [the CI] on as soon as I wake up. I also don't like to wear it when I'm sick with a cold or the flu. No one likes to hear themselves when they are like that. And sometimes I don't wear it because I just like the silence . . . no distractions."

With regard to advising parents to choose cochlear implant surgery for their deaf child Kyler explains, "It depends on the parents. If they are mostly a hearing family and they want the child to be more a part of the hearing world, then I would get the CI surgery as soon as possible because the younger, the easier it is . . . before their [child's] language is set." With regard to Deaf parents, Kyler replied, "Well, if they're part of the Deaf world, they probably won't 'fix' their kid's hearing unless they want their child to interpret for them or help them communicate with hearing people. Most likely they won't. Most Deaf parents have hearing children anyway."

On the subject of teaching all young children sign language Kyler becomes emphatic: "I think all kids, no matter if they're hearing or deaf, should learn sign language. It's such a visual thing! Younger kids can't put things into words right away, so sign language is a way to help them communicate faster and easier. It [research] shows that signs have a positive effect on young children."

At the End of the Day, What Is Important?

As parents, if asked what is important, we might say that we want our children to be literate, academically successful, independent, able to pursue their dreams, think their own thoughts, be happy and well adjusted, capable, confident . . . be successful (whatever that might entail), lead meaningful lives, be at peace with themselves and others. As educators we might say very much the same thing about our students, except we would, of course, add that we want them to be lifelong learners. The truth of the matter is that quite possibly all we wish for our progeny may hinge on whether they like themselves . . . that they like who they are and would not desire to be any other way.

As my interviews with Ginny, Bob, and Kyler (which spanned the course of three years) were coming to a conclusion I realized that I had never directly asked Kyler how she felt about herself. Although Kyler makes statements such as "I like the way I am . . . I'm happy my parents chose a cochlear implant for me . . . it allows me to function better," I was not sure those comments told the full story, and I was not sure how to get at the heart of the matter utilizing an interview format.

It is important to highlight the fact that deaf education professionals have expressed considerable concern about the potential for implanted children to fare poorly in terms of developing a positive sense of self. They maintain that these children would not have an opportunity to develop sign language proficiency and experience Deaf enculturation (Crouch, 1997; Lane & Grodin, 1997). These notions were among the concerns expressed by the teacher from the school for deaf children when she phoned Ginny the day before Kyler's scheduled implant surgery. Sparrow (2005) further delineates the concerns as follows:

> The danger with existing cochlear implants is that they risk depriving such children of full membership of *any* culture.

Implantees may end up trapped "between cultures," unable to function effectively in a hearing context but also lacking the facility with sign language available to those who grow up with it as their first language. (pp. 143–44)

In 2012 researchers Spencer, Tomblin, and Bruce published a paper titled "Growing Up with a Cochlear Implant: Education, Vocation, and Affiliation." They utilized the Satisfaction with Life Scale (SWLS; Diener et al., 1985) and the Deaf Identity Scale (Weinberg & Sterritt, 1986) to obtain affiliation and quality-of-life data from a cohort of children with bilateral, profound hearing loss who had received cochlear implants under a study funded by the National Institutes of Health. Educational and vocational outcomes were collected from user survey data. I decided to follow the same format with Kyler in order to elicit a self-assessment of her quality of life.

Table 1. Items from the Satisfaction with Life Scale

Statements to Score	
1. In most ways, my life is close to my ideal.	**Kyler's response: 5**
2. The conditions of my life are excellent.	**Kyler's response: 6**
3. I am satisfied with my life.	**Kyler's response: 5**
4. So far I have gotten the important things I want in life.	**Kyler's response: 6**
5. If I could live my life over, I would change almost nothing.	**Kyler's response: 6**

Kyler was asked to read each statement and rate her level of agreement using a 1–7 scale, where a rating of "1" indicates strong disagreement and "7" indicates strong agreement. The rating breakdown is as follows: 1 (strongly disagree); 2 (disagree); 3 (disagree somewhat); 4 (undecided); 5 (agree somewhat); 6 (agree);

7 (strongly agree). The mean subscale score for the respondents in the Spencer et al. (2012) study was 5.9, indicating that CI respondents report a high level of satisfaction with life: 4 points higher than the mean of college undergraduates in the study by Diener et al. (1985).

Kyler's mean score is 5.6, which is one point higher than the mean for college undergraduates. When asked about the scores assigned to questions 1 and 3, Kyler responds as follows:

> I dreamed of being a vet, horse trainer, or zookeeper . . . pretty much anything with animals . . . getting to work with them and allowing that interaction to inspire my artwork was my goal. I am happy working as a registered vet tech; wages are less than teaching, but happiness is more valuable to me. At the same time, I feel guilty that I'm not working in a job that relates more to my art degrees. My options related to an art career are limited in this area. I'm currently satisfied with my life . . . just on the fence about what long-term job to pursue. No matter what that is, I will always be involved in art because it is a big part of what makes me . . . ME!"

In order to assess affiliation patterns of identity, Spencer et al. administered the Deaf Identity Scale developed by Weinberg and Sterritt (1986). A true/false response to the statements was required of respondents (see table 2).

Table 2. The Deaf Identity Subscale Items

Hearing Identification Subscale	
I would rather have hearing friends.	**Kyler's response: F**
I am more like hearing people than deaf people.	**Kyler's response: F**
One day I will be able to hear.	**Kyler's response: F**
When I get married, it will be to a hearing person.	**Kyler's response: T**
I like people to think I am hearing.	**Kyler's response: T**

Deaf Identification Subscale	
I would rather have only deaf friends.	**Kyler's response: F**
In the future, I hope to have only deaf neighbors.	**Kyler's response: F**
I'd rather be around deaf people only.	**Kyler's response: F**
When I work, I hope it is around deaf people only.	**Kyler's response: F**
When I get married, it will be to a deaf person.	**Kyler's response: F**

Dual Identification Subscale	
It's important to have both hearing and deaf friends.	**Kyler's response: T**
It doesn't matter if I work around deaf or hearing people or both.	**Kyler's response: T**
It doesn't matter if I work around deaf or hearing people or both.	**Kyler's response: T**
I would rather have both deaf and hearing friends.	**Kyler's response: T**
When I have children, I don't care if they are deaf or hearing.	**Kyler's response: T**

In the Spencer et al. study, 87% of the respondents endorsed a primary dual identification, and 79% of the respondents endorsed all of the items from the Dual Identity scale. Kyler's highest endorsement ranking was given to a dual identity, an indication that she feels equally comfortable with both Deaf individuals and hearing individuals. Weinberg and Sterritt (1986) found that endorsing a dual identity was linked with better outcomes in academic placement, social relationships, personal adjustment, and perceived family acceptance than was the endorsement of a Deaf identity or a hearing identity. Both the findings of Spencer et al. (2012)

and Weinberg and Sterritt (1986) indicate that CI users express a high satisfaction with life, high rates of postsecondary education, and an elevated tendency to support dual identity. These findings diminish concerns that profoundly deaf individuals growing up with cochlear implants will become culturally isolated and unable to function in either the hearing or the Deaf world. In Kyler's case, her responses support the notion that she has good self-acceptance, feels comfortable with and confident in herself, and feels equally comfortable with d/Deaf and hearing individuals.

Summary

By all accounts Kyler is an intelligent, artistic, athletic, young woman with an engaging personality and a strong sense of self. Kyler's life has not been one consumed entirely by her own wants and needs, as is exemplified by her involvement in volunteerism and service to others. She achieved academic success throughout her public school endeavors, continued to be successful as a college student, and remains so in the world of work. Artistically, she is gifted and has professional aspirations. She is a young "deaf" woman who benefits from a cochlear implant but requires an interpreter and a note taker in order to successfully access information provided in an academic environment. She does not consider herself to be defined by her deafness but sees it rather as "just a part of who I am." In short, Kyler typifies what society considers a "well-rounded" young adult, one who has much to share with those around her and with society at large.

Historically, the field of Deaf education has been plagued by controversy over methodology and ideology and has struggled with a legacy of "lost potential" regarding less than satisfactory student achievement. Additionally, the profession has grappled with providing equal rights for d/Deaf individuals in authority and leadership roles. It was only after the historic "Deaf President

Now" movement (1988) at Gallaudet University, when students took control of the university campus, that the right to determine administrative control of their educational institution was gained. Shortly thereafter (1990), Deaf individuals began to address practices that give access to the curriculum by focusing on a bicultural-bilingual approach to instruction.

However, certain choices concerning how one deals with deafness are met with intolerance. Common in the field of Deaf education is the maintenance of a strongly held conviction about how one should respond to deafness; typically it is a "one size fits all" approach. We have tended to pursue the concept that all deaf children should be educated under a single philosophical umbrella even though we universally recognize the fact that children are diverse and therefore benefit differently from varying auditory and visual stimuli (some more, some less, others not at all). Such thinking is often driven by bias, which can arise from different sources, one of which is group egotism that occurs when the group with whom one identifies assumes that its ideals are correct and those of others are not. Philosopher Bernard Lonergan (1957) points out that bias blocks development and stifles understanding and acceptance. Bias is limiting in that it prevents one from crossing boundaries and promotes the tendency to remain solidly behind the line that has been drawn in the sand. It can create a predisposition to close off opportunities to expand personal horizons. Bias creates an ocean of losses that leaves those who are entrenched in their biases in a philosophical camp incapable of benefiting from the wisdom and unity that are born of diversity and freedom of choice.

Chapter 7

Lessons Learned: A Cautionary Tale

In looking at relationships among schools, teachers, audiologists, surgeons, and families several noteworthy experiences call to mind the importance of treating families and their children in the most respectful manner possible. On occasion we professionals can become such zealots in our philosophical and educational beliefs that we have the potential to influence and/or manipulate decisions that parents alone should make. The responsibility to educate and make available all of the possible options for the d/Deaf child is that of the professional; the final decisions about surgical options and educational methods rest with the parents.

The importance of a sense of security that comes as a result of parental/familial acceptance of a child born deaf—born with unanticipated challenges—cannot be minimized. Nor can the security that results from an embracing, nurturing, and academically stimulating educational environment be underestimated. The sense of belonging created by a community of acceptance, whether it be found in playing a team sport, involvement in the fine arts, volunteerism, participation in a church community, or any combination of these and other such activities promotes a sense of well-being—a sense of accomplishment, the ability to give and share—the ability to see oneself as having a vital role in the world in which we live.

Finally, there is the hope that we as parents, educators, and professionals hold for our children, which is that they will be able to build bridges, cross barriers, and gain independence of thought, ambition, and resolve. A goal that each of us can embrace is that our students and children will emerge from their time with us able to attain the highest measure of their capabilities, to be productive members of society who have a positive sense of self, and to influence all with whom they come into contact.

I and Thou

Martin Buber (1875–1965), a philosopher and theologian, wrote a book titled *I and Thou*, a work that sought to get at the heart of human relations. In his book Buber describes the notion that individuals relate to others and identify with the outside world in two primary ways. He characterized the first as an objective relationship that he termed "I-It." In such a relationship, one views what is outside oneself in a purely objective manner, as a thing to be manipulated for selfish purposes. Simply put, people are viewed as objects to be controlled (Ozmon & Craver, 2008).

Buber refers to the second type of relationship as "I-Thou," in which individuals have an intense, personal world of meaning. In such a scenario people treat one another with mutual respect and value. Buber was one of the few existentialists who wrote specifically about education, in particular about the nature of the relationship between teacher and student. His goal was the establishment of an educational setting where teacher and student, though differing in type and depth of knowledge, were on equal footing in terms of their humanity and ability to learn from one another (Ozmon & Craver, 2008). The relationships illuminated in the Daniels' family story reveal multiple examples of "I-Thou" relationships, which are readily identifiable.

There are, as well, at least two examples of Buber's "I-It" relationships that were recorded. They occur in tandem. The first is exemplified by the phone call Ginny received at work, from a teacher at the school for deaf children the day before Kyler's implant surgery. The teacher urged Ginny to cancel the surgery and allow Kyler to make that decision herself when she became old enough to fully appreciate its implications.

The second occurred when members of the cochlear implant team encouraged Ginny to stop signing with Kyler at home and phase out signing in Kyler's educational environment. In both scenarios seemingly well-intentioned individuals attempted to control or influence Ginny's decisions based on their own philosophy of education and intervention rather than honoring Ginny's hard-reached decision.

Missing in the two experiences are the elements of respect and appreciation for Ginny's research, interviews with other parents who had chosen implants for their children, Kyler's success in the use of sign language, its underlying benefits for her, and Ginny's commitment to a harmonious blending of successful language use and medical technology. In each case, the professionals felt that they knew better than the parents what was best for Kyler and felt compelled to foist their opinion on the family rather than ask how Ginny and Bob had reached their decisions and inquire how they as professionals could support the family.

Buber further hypothesized that a series of "I-Thou" relationships constitute a continuum with humanity at one end and God at the other. He believed that the divine and the human are related and that, through communication with humankind, one would experience a shared partisanship that would stimulate spiritual bonds. Faith in God and in humankind was the basis of Buber's belief in a greater good, a good beyond that of the individual (Ozmon & Craver 2008, p. 227).

Such values are evident in Ginny's pursuit of a spiritual connection, a pursuit that would give purpose to Kyler's deafness.

Ginny acknowledges that her seemingly struggle-free acceptance of Kyler's deafness was most likely the result of two conditions: the first was that her "career as a caregiver for individuals with disabilities helped her accept this challenge," and the second was the result of believing "that God chose me to be Kyler's mom because I could deal with her deafness. My belief is that God is in control, no matter what happens, and He will get us through."

This idea is echoed by Kyler, who sees her deafness as contributing to a purpose: "I think He [God] created each one of us special, and He decided to make me deaf to bring a change on Mom's life, a positive, necessary [change] . . . not negative."

Interestingly, at one point in the interview Kyler refers to her deafness as a "gift" that allows her to have advantages not enjoyed by others, like being able to turn off her implant receiver in noisy situations and being able to enjoy the sound of silence.

Reflected in these comments by Ginny and Kyler is the recognition of a sense of divine purpose in their lives and the resulting ability to accept what might ordinarily be considered a challenge as a "gift." The notion put forth by Buber—that the divine and the human are connected—does not negate the certainty of struggle but rather gives hope that struggles can stimulate opportunities as well as fuel the ability to overcome the difficulties. Ginny, Bob, and Kyler are persons who have been challenged by what was for them an unknown. Their individual journeys led each, via different paths, to recognize and appreciate the positive outcomes of their situation. Such is suggested by Bob's reflection: "To be honest, we've grown into better people."

Mentoring: Life in the Red Tent

The majority of Kyler's time in the public schools was spent in the company of three women who were her primary teachers from pre-K through grade eight. I doubt there is an educator who would at first blush find this to be a suitable educational scenario. My own concern was that such a circumstance was at the very least educationally limiting. It was my belief that deaf children in the public school system should be integrated for instruction and that instruction should be preceded and followed by concept expansion and discussion via the educator of the d/Deaf students. When a student was found to be unsuccessful, most likely a better and more appropriate placement would be at a school for deaf children. Such a placement would then provide the student with a variety of teachers who were both skilled in sign language and knowledgeable with regard to their subject matter.

Anita Diamant's *The Red Tent* (1997) is a novel about women of Hebrew heritage predating the birth of Christ. The title refers to the tent in which the women reside during their "time of the month" or while giving birth. In the confines of the tent, the young women learned from other women what it is to be female, what it is to be a Hebrew, and what it is to bring forth life. It was a cocooned environment that prepared them for life in their larger environs.

As I have poured over Kyler's academic work, educational and audiological evaluations, speech and language reports, and curriculum content, it has become apparent to me that she was a successful student. With that in mind, it is impossible not to give greater thought to what occurred during the ten years with Kyler's primary teaching staff of three women. The majority of Kyler's curriculum was accessed in her small classroom, she was educated by women in the company of five and sometimes six other girls and one boy. Kyler's elementary school principal was a woman, as were her audiologist, speech pathologist, and interpreter. In middle school, the teaching ratio diminished to three staff persons working with four students.

Kyler was surrounded by strong, intelligent, female role models at home, at school, at church, and at athletic events. She was nurtured, mentored, and educated by women in the "womb" of home and classroom. Because of Kyler's ability to function in the greater society, one can only surmise that her time in the cocooned environment was not a period of imposed limitations but rather one of rich growth and development. This scenario speaks, nay shouts, of the importance of nurturing, mentoring, and educating within the "red tent," where one is unreservedly accepted as a whole and unique being, where the rhythms of life and learning lend a sense of comfort and predictability and equip for a time when one will be thrust into the classroom of the world, which is often less accepting, encouraging, and forgiving.

Building Bridges, Crossing Borders

In the book *Translated Woman* (1993), Ruth Behar crosses the border between the United States and Mexico for a number of years to document the story of a Hispanic woman named Esperanza. Behar comes to use the term *border crossing* for more than crossing a physical boundary. She includes in her concept those boundaries that ethnic minorities, women, and/or other disenfranchised groups must cross to gain entry or access to a variety of opportunities such as education, knowledge, and an expanded worldview. These are experiences the dominant culture enjoys seemingly without effort, without the necessity of crossing a border. In the case of Ruth Behar and Esperanza and in most scenarios addressing disenfranchised persons and those who bring their plight to life, their real and symbolic border crossings are mutually beneficial and yield unanticipated discoveries.

In the field of education, we, too, have borders. There are professional boundaries between teacher and student. Often there is no crossing of the borders that exist between professional and personal life. Our families typically do not interact with our students' families; our students generally do not interact with their teachers outside the classroom.

However, in contemplating Kyler's educational experience, that is clearly not the case. Border crossings may have existed for a variety of reasons: the limitations imposed by living in a small community, difficulty in recruiting professionals from outside the area, or a combination of these and other factors. Whatever the reason, the fact remains that Kyler enjoyed a unique relationship with her teaching staff over the 10-year period they worked together. Throughout elementary school, a daily journal traveled from home to school and back. There were numerous gatherings of students, teachers, and their families throughout the 10-year span via invitations to get together in the classroom and invitations to gather in one another's homes. As with Ruth and Esperanza, the border crossings enjoyed by Kyler, her classmates, and the teaching staff were mutually beneficial because they allowed for a multitude of shared experiences and expansion of knowledge.

My relationship with Kyler and Ginny, if diagrammed, might look somewhat like a spiderweb with our lives being connected by threads of friendship, faith, deafness, sign language, mentoring, interpreting, teaching, learning, observing, and living. Such border crossings have enriched my life beyond measure. I have benefited from a wonderful friendship and have had the privilege of watching a child grow into adulthood while mastering the use of a cochlear implant, engaging in distinctive ways with society at large, and providing me with unique ways of seeing the world through eyes not my own.

Kyler has crossed the borders of language acquisition by learning to communicate via sign language, discriminate and interpret information received electronically through her implant, communicate with people who do not know sign language, and navigate in a society made up primarily of a hearing/speaking population. Most critically, Kyler has not allowed herself to be defined by delineations or boundaries arbitrarily determined by others. As a result, she has achieved a life rich with possibilities.

Ginny crossed the borders of motherhood by parenting a deaf child, embracing sign language, and becoming an advocate for her daughter until Kyler became old enough to become her own advocate. She also mastered the building of bridges across borders of controversy, thus establishing the right for Kyler to determine her own identity, that of a person who has a strong sense of who she is, one who is academically successful, loves listening to music and going to concerts, and is not defined by her deafness.

Bob crossed borders of entry into fatherhood and dwelt in a land filled with anger after learning of Kyler's deafness. He confessed his descent into the bottle as an escape from his fear of the unknown, not to mention trepidation about cochlear implant surgery. His final crossing from "no man's land" into the reality of acceptance was achieved as he became reconciled to what was possible for Kyler. Bob terms this gradual dawning "a learning experience," which consisted of the melting away of the raw emotions that haunted him as he watched Kyler grow, learn, achieve, thrive, and succeed.

For those of us, whether as educators, speech therapists, interpreters, audiologists, or medical professionals, who had the honor of crossing the border into the lived experience of Ginny, Bob, and Kyler, our lives have been made richer. We are professionals who became learners because we were taught by a beneficent mother, father, and daughter.

Were border crossings to be embraced in the field of Deaf education, its result would be to eliminate the entrenched camps of exclusivity among those who espouse oral, Total

Communication, or bilingual-bicultural philosophies. It would create for "deaf" and "Deaf" children and their families the freedom to be well informed about the various options available and provide opportunities to help them choose from an accessible developmental, philosophical, and academic menu (without imposed guilt or recrimination) what is best for each child, each family, and each cultural identity. Merv Garretson, former Gallaudet University faculty member who is himself Deaf (1995, p. 51) describes such a process: "Let us prepare teachers who are impartial, not dogmatic, who do not run away from controversial issues but do justice to all sides, rise above biased thinking and encourage open discussion. We must stop looking at deafness in a narrow, isolationist sense but as a component part of our respective native countries."

Reflections

The original title of what began as a dissertation evolved as the writing progressed. Initially the title was "In Midstream: Exploring the Life of a Young Deaf Woman and Her Evolution." In "midstream" because Ginny's, Bob's, and Kyler's lives were not carried out in the mainstream, the conventional, ordinary way, the way that allows life's circumstances to direct its course. Theirs has been a life lived "midstream," not standing on the banks of timidity but plunging headlong into the current, sometimes enjoying the rush of exhilaration that comes with the white water of enjoyed success and at other times swimming against the current that is representative of decisions made other than those desired by professionals. "In Midstream" was a keeper, but . . . there was more than evolution involved, although that is certainly a part of the story.

It was followed by "In Midstream: A Qualitative Case Study of a Young Deaf Woman, Medical and Academic Decisions, and Their Life-Changing Impact." At that point in the writing it seemed that Kyler's entire story could be reduced to a series of isolated decisions and the impact that each had on her life. Perhaps the outcome would be a sort of handbook one that if followed by parents and professionals might result in, other deaf children benefiting and enjoying the same kinds of successes experienced by Kyler. Her story could be packaged and tied up with a neat little bow to be imitated far and wide.

The truth is, however, that despite my anticipation of being able to isolate decisions and choices that contributed to Kyler's success, it was not to be. I could not draw yet another philosophical or methodological line in the sand that maintained a certain prescriptive scenario that would, if followed, result in all deaf children becoming emotionally, academically, and physically successful. That would be the antithesis of all that has been learned from this remarkable family. The title then became "In Midstream: A Qualitative Case Study of a Young Deaf Woman—Becoming 'Kyler'." This work, if anything, is one that frames the story of a young woman who has come of age, is able to define and embrace her self, and is comfortable with who she is and who she will become. Finally, as a book, the title has morphed into *Building Bridges, Crossing Borders,* which recognizes the importance of collaboration among professionals and families of "deaf" and "Deaf" children and of providing opportunities to select from an array of "bridge"-building materials, with the goal in each case of allowing for acceptance of oneself and acceptance by one's family, academic success, and the ability to cross borders and boundaries previously imposed by others.

Kyler's undeniably positive sense of self seems to be at the core of all else. When asked, "Where do you get your sense of self-worth?" Kyler responded simply, "Mainly from my mother and her faith. She was sure things would work out. I guess I got that positive attitude from her; faith probably had a lot to do with it." There was no effort on Kyler's part to attribute her sense of self-worth to the use of a cochlear implant, sign language, public school attendance, fitting in with hearing and deaf classmates, or the development of intelligible speech and good auditory discrimination skills. She did not single out a friend or a teacher who was instrumental in formulating the notion that "We are all special."

Certainly, what is important for every child is to feel loved and valued and to gain a sense of who they are in the cosmos. As Kyler noted, "He [God] decided to make me special, and He made sure that He gave me to parents who would accept me and not give me up for adoption like some parents would . . . or get rid of me." This statement reflects a deep sense of security with regard to her parents and their acceptance, and it is contrasted with what is, in Kyler's mind, the unthinkable, that parents might want to "get rid of me."

There is a long-standing concern that if a young deaf child receives a cochlear implant, the child will feel rejected because he or she will believe that deafness is something that needs to be "fixed." There is a fear that a sense of not being good enough "as is" will be instilled in the implant recipient as a result of the surgically "corrective" procedure (see Christiansen & Leigh, 2002; Weisberg, et al., 2000; Padden & Humphries, 2005). There is little doubt that such concerns are legitimate and are central to a fear of rejection, which is common to most members of society, whether hearing or deaf. I am particularly sensitive to the fear of the loss of language, culture, and heritage as these apply to the Deaf members of our society and insofar as inclusive educational settings and medical intervention may lead to an ethnic cleansing of sorts, a silent genocide of those who are linguistically different. It is a sentiment that cannot be ignored, yet one that cannot presume to rule the decisions of hearing parents who give birth to children who cannot hear. Such are the concerns and considerations that result in the philosophical polarization in the field of deaf education, which is characterized by an ideology that finds one attitude to be correct and all others to be erroneous and somehow—even blasphemous.

The purpose of this undertaking was to gain new insights by exploring decisions made on Kyler's behalf, including the choice to use sign language, embrace a cochlear implant, access speech therapy pre-K through grade 12, and pursue public school placement. The attainment of newly gained insights has been achieved, albeit not the insights I expected at the outset. I am reminded of researcher/author Sharon Merriam's conception of what might be wrought through qualitative research or living with others: "Being open to any possibility can lead to serendipitous discoveries" (1998, p. 121). The fact that spending extended periods of time with students and their families can be transformative is beyond question, for it provides a vehicle for understanding not only others but oneself as well . . . accessing insights that might otherwise remain forever veiled.

What has been learned after living with the narrative of this family over time is that reflection and/or contemplation do not quickly bring about understanding or theoretical and philosophical formulations and solutions; rather, understanding comes slowly, latently, and in quiet moments after much toil among the lived experiences of those we attempt to teach and come to know.

Considerations and Implications

In an article titled "Language Planning for the 21st Century: Revisiting Bilingual Language Policy for Deaf Children" (2012), authors Harry Knoors and Marc Marschark acknowledge the need for a reexamination of language planning and policy.

This need, they hold, springs from the widespread use of universal newborn hearing screening, the recent growth in the use of technological developments such as digital hearing aids and cochlear implants and their resulting potential for young deaf children to develop spoken language. I recently heard Michael Chorost, author of the book *Rebuilt: My Journey Back to the Hearing World* (2005), speak at a state conference on deafness. He made a statement that I found most interesting: "Deafness is not generalizable." This is precisely the same conclusion reached by Knoors and Marschark, who advise that language policies be revisited to ensure "they are appropriate for the increasingly diverse population of deaf children (p. 291)." Hearing parents are tending more and more to pursue use of technology in addressing their child's deafness, while the birth through college-age population of children and young adults no longer comprises only d/Deaf individuals who are either utilizing hearings aids . . . or not and/or choosing to embrace sign language or not. We have, instead, parents of d/Deaf children who are choosing to access language and education by means of an array of options and, as a result, young d/Deaf adults desiring to make use of a range of options, of whom Kyler is representative.

Paludneviciene and Leigh, editors of *Cochlear Implants: Evolving Perspectives,* indicate that some deaf parents are expressing a desire for more: "not only do they want their children to be academically successful and linguistically fluent in ASL and written English, but they also want their children to be competent users of spoken English" (2011, p. 72). The belief expressed by deaf parents who have chosen to have their deaf children implanted is that their children will have the same opportunities as their hearing peers. This echoes the sentiment that parents, by and large, want their children to break down barriers (including those that the parents themselves have found to be limiting), thus creating greater opportunities to access all that is available. What is becoming increasingly obvious is that we cannot presume to determine which parents may choose the option of a cochlear implant for their deaf child; it is not generalizable to a single subgroup but rather is a trend that is gaining momentum among hearing and deaf parents alike, around the globe and throughout the entire range of socioeconomic levels.

Knoors and Marschark (2012) indicate that their once strongly held position with regard to the necessity of pursuing a bilingual-bicultural linguistic and educational model for young deaf children has been modified in recent years, a fact that they attribute to the widespread use of universal hearing screening at birth, the enormous increase in the number of children receiving implants at increasingly young ages, and the resulting improvements in hearing and speech (e.g., Dettman & Dowell, 2010; Hammer, 2010; Verbist, 2010). Knoors and Marschark (2012) frame the issue of revisiting language planning and policy in deaf education not from a political or philosophical perspective but rather as a need that has arisen in response to providing an increasingly diverse population of "deaf children with the best possible opportunities for educational and personal success" (p. 292).

It is incumbent upon professionals in the fields of deaf education, audiology, and otolaryngology to be well informed of current medical technology, research, and the resulting educational, psychosocial, and emotional outcomes. Of equal importance is the need for open, honest, and reflective dialogue to occur at universities and teacher preparation facilities in an effort to address the transitions occurring in Deaf education as a result of technological developments and research. It is critical in turn to allow those findings to drive all that is needed to develop and provide differentiated instruction to meet the diverse needs of today's d/Deaf population from early childhood through the completion of college and/or technical training.

Critical are the implications for teacher training in terms of emphasis on the importance of respecting and supporting family relationships, which in turn serve to support and stimulate positive self-esteem, academic skills, and social-emotional well-being (see Petitto, 1993; Calderon, 2000; Calderon & Greenberg, 2003). Consideration should be given to the implementation of curricular planning in teacher and interpreter training programs that would introduce coursework on mentoring and its ethical implications, particularly as it applies to deaf students in inclusive educational settings.

In conclusion, it is most fitting to quote from the preface of Dr. Elliott Eisner's revolutionary text, *The Educational Imagination*. His sentiment, embodies ideals that if taken to heart could yield the greatest opportunity for educational success for the student population at large as well as to the future generations of d/Deaf and hard of hearing students.

> If there is one idea that permeates these pages, it is the belief that no single educational program is appropriate for all children, everywhere, forever. Which educational values are appropriate for children and adolescents depends on the characteristics of those the program is designed to serve, the features of the context in which they live, and the values that they and the community embrace. Further, these values and this context itself is likely to change over time. Looked at this way, the practice of education is a dynamic one, subject to change over time. This means that educators cannot rest with fixed solutions to educational problems or with "break-throughs" that once and for all define or prescribe how and what should be done. Ours is a practical enterprise, and practical enterprises elude fixed solutions. (2002, p. v)

References

Adler, P. A. & Adler, P. (1994). Observational techniques. In N. K. Denzin & Y. S. Lincoln (Eds.), *Handbook of qualitative research* (pp. 377–392). Thousand Oaks, CA: Sage.

Arnos, K. & Pandya, A. (2003). Advances in the genetics of deafness. In M. Marschark & P. E. Spencer (Eds.), *Oxford handbook of deaf studies, language, and education* (pp. 392–405). New York, NY: Oxford University Press.

Aronson, J. (Director), Weisberg, R. (Producer), Roth, J. (Producer), & Sacks, J. (Producer). *Sound and fury* [Motion picture]. United States: Artistic License.

Baker, C., & Cokely, D. (1980). *American Sign Language: A teacher's resource text on grammar and culture.* Silver Spring, MD: TJ Publishers.

Bavelier, D. & Neville, H. J. (2002). Cross-modal plasticity: Where and how? *Nat. Rev. Neurosci. 3,* 443–452.

Behar, R. (1993). *Translated woman: Crossing the border with Esperanza's story.* Boston, MA: Beacon Press.

Blamey, P., Arndt, P., Bergeron, F., Bredberg, G., Brimacombe, J., Facer, G., Larky, J., Lindstrom, B., Nedzelski, J., Perterson, A., Shipp, D., Staller, S., & Whitford, L. (1996). Factors affecting auditory performance of postlinguistically deaf adults using cochlear implants. *Audiology and Neurotology, 1,* 293–306.

Bornstein, H., Saulnier, K., & Hamilton, L. B. (1983). *The comprehensive signed English dictionary.* Washington, DC: Gallaudet University Press.

Calderon, R. (2000). Parental involvement in deaf children's education programs as a predictor of child's language, early reading, and social emotional development. *Journal of Deaf Studies and Deaf Education, 5,* 140–155.

Calderon, R., & Greenberg, M. T. (1997). The effectiveness of early intervention for deaf children and children with hearing loss. In M. J. Guralnick (Ed.), *The effectiveness of early intervention* (pp. 455–482). Baltimore, MD: Paul H. Brookes.

Calderon, R., & Greenberg, M. T. (1999). Stress and coping in hearing mothers with children with hearing loss: Factors affecting mother and child adjustment. *American Annals of the Deaf, 144,* 7–18.

Calderon, R., & Greenberg, M. T. (2000). Challenges to parents and professionals in promoting socioemotional development in Deaf children. In P. E. Spencer, C. J. Erting, & M. Marschark (Eds.), *The deaf child in the family and at school* (pp. 167–185). Mahwah, NJ: Lawrence Erlbaum Associates.

Calderon, R., & Greenberg, M. T. (2003). Social and emotional development of Deaf children: Family, school and program effects. In M. Marschark & P. E. Spencer (Eds.), *Oxford handbook of deaf studies, language, and education* (pp. 177–189). New York, NY: Oxford University Press.

Charmaz, K. (2005). Grounded theory in the twenty-first century: Applications for advancing social justice studies. In N. K. Denzin & Y. S. Lincoln (Eds.), *The handbook of qualitative research* (pp. 507–535). Thousand Oaks, CA: Sage.

Cambourne, B. (1990). Beyond the deficit theory: A 1990's perspective on literacy failure. *Australian Journal of Reading, 13*(4), 289–299.

Chorost, M. (2005). *Rebuilt: My journey back to the hearing world.* Boston, MA: Houghton Mifflin.

Christiansen, J., & Leigh, I. (2002). *Cochlear implants in children: Ethics and choices.* Washington, DC: Gallaudet University Press.

Cohen, D., & Harrison, M. (1982). *The curriculum action project: A report of curriculum decision making in Australian schools.* Sydney, Australia: Macquarie University.

Commission on the Education of the Deaf. (1988). *Toward equality: Education of the deaf. A report to the President and the Congress of the United States.* Washington, DC: U.S. Government Printing Office.

Connor, C. M. (2006). Examining the communication skills of a young cochlear implant pioneer. *Journal of Deaf Studies and Deaf Education, 11*(4), 449–460.

Connor, C. M., & Zwolan, T. A. (2004). Examining multiple sources of influence on the reading comprehension skills of children who use cochlear implants. *Journal of Speech, Language and Hearing Research, 47,* 509–526.

Crouch, R. A. (1997). Letting the deaf be deaf—Reconsidering the use of cochlear implantation in prelingually deaf children. *Hastings Center Report 27*(4), 14–21.

Davis, J. (1974). Performance of young hearing-impaired children on a test of basic concepts. *Journal of Speech & Hearing Research, 17,* 342–351.

Denzin, N. K., & Lincoln, Y. S. (2005). *The sage handbook of qualitative research,* (3rd ed.). Thousand Oaks, CA: Sage.

Denzin, N. K., & Lincoln, Y. S. (2005). Introduction: The discipline and practice of qualitative research. In N. K. Denzin & Y. S. Lincoln (Eds.), *The handbook of qualitative research* (pp. 1–32). Thousand Oaks, CA: Sage.

Dettman, S., & Dowell, R. (2010). Language acquisition and critical periods for children using cochlear implants. The demands of writing and the deaf writer. In M. Marschark & P. E. Spencer (Eds.), *The Oxford handbook of deaf studies, language, and education* (Vol. 2, pp. 331–342). New York: Oxford University Press.

Diamant, A. (1997). *The red tent.* Atlanta, GA: Chalice Press.

Diener, E., Emmons, R., Larsen, R., & Griffin, S. (1985). The Satisfaction with Life Scale. *Journal of Personality Assessment, 49*(1), 71–78.

Dorman, M. F., & Wilson, B. S. (2004). The design and function of cochlear implants. *American Scientist, 92*, 436–445.

Edwards, B. (1999). *The new drawing on the left side of the brain.* New York, NY: Penguin Putnam.

Eisner, E. W. (2002). *The educational imagination: On the design and evaluation of school programs.* Upper Saddle River, NJ: Merrill Prentice Hall.

Erting, C. J. (1992). Deafness and literacy: Why can't Sam read? *Sign Language Studies, 7*, 97–112.

Fant, L. J., Jr. (1972). *Ameslan: An introduction to American Sign Language.* Silver Spring, MD: National Association of the Deaf.

Ferris, C. (1980). *A hug just isn't enough.* Washington, DC: Gallaudet College Press.

Fontana, A., & Frey, J. H. (1994). Interviewing: The art of science. In N. K. Denzin & Y. S. Lincoln (Eds.), *The handbook of qualitative research* (pp. 361–376). Thousand Oaks, CA: Sage.

Freire, P. (2007). *Pedagogy of the oppressed.* (30th anniversary ed.). New York, NY: Continuum.

Gallaway, C. (1998). Early interaction. In S. Gregory, P. Knight, W. McCracken, S. Power, & L. Watson (Eds.), *Issues in deaf education* (pp. 49–57). London: Fulton.

Gannon, J. R. (1981). *Deaf heritage: A narrative history of deaf America.* Silver Spring, MD: National Association of the Deaf.

Gannon, J. R. (1989). *The week the world heard Gallaudet.* Washington, DC: Gallaudet University Press.

Gantz, B. J., Woodworth, G. G., Kuntson, J. F., Abbas, P. J., & Tyler, R. S. (1993). Multivariate predictors of audiological success with multichannel cochlear implants. *Annals of Otology, Rhinology, and Laryngology, 102*, 909–916.

Garman, N. (1994, 5 August). Qualitative inquiry: Meaning and menace for educational researchers. Paper presented at the Qualitative Approaches in Educational Research conference, Flinders University of South Australia.

Garretson, M. (1995). When tomorrow comes: A challenge to educators of deaf children. *Deafness: Life & Culture II, A Deaf American Monograph*, 45, 49–53.

Geers, A. E., Kuehn, G., & Moog, J. S. (1981). EPIC: Experimental project in the instructional concentration: Evaluation and results. *American Annals of the Deaf*, 126(8), 929–964.

Geers, A., & Schick, B. (1988). Acquisition of spoken and signed English by hearing-impaired children of hearing-impaired or hearing parents. *Journal of Speech and Hearing Research*, 53(2), 136–143.

Geers, A. E. (2002). Factors affecting the development of speech, language, and literacy in children with early cochlear implantation. *Language, Speech, and Hearing Services in Schools*, 33, 172–183.

Giezen, M. R. (2011). *Speech and sign perception in deaf children with cochlear implants.* (PhD dissertation). University of Amsterdam. LOT Dissertational Series 275. Retrieved from http://www.lotpublications.nl.

Grosjean, F. (1992). The bilingual and the bicultural person in the Hearing and in the Deaf world. *Sign Language Studies*, 77, 307–320.

Gurian, A., & Goodman, R. F. (2011). How important are the first three years of a baby's life? An interview with David Steinberg. *The Child Study Center.* Retrieved from http://www.aboutourkids.org/articles/how_important_are_first_three_years_baby039s_life.

Hammer, A. (2010). *The acquisition of verbal morphology in cochlear-implanted and specific language impaired children.* (PhD dissertation). Retrieved from http://www.lotpublications.nl.

Hoemann, H. W. (1976). *The American Sign Language: Lexical and grammatical notes with translation exercises.* Silver Spring, MD: National Association of the Deaf.

Huberman, A. M., & Miles, M. B. (1983). Drawing valid meaning from qualitative data: Some techniques of data reduction and display. *Quality and Quantity, 17*(4), 281–339.

Innes, J. J. (1994). Full inclusion and the deaf student: A deaf consumer's review of the issue. *American Annals of the Deaf, 139*(2), 152–156.

Johnson, R. E., Liddell, S. K., & Erting, C. J. (1989). *Unlocking the curriculum: Principles for achieving access in deaf education.* (Gallaudet Research Institute Working Paper 89 no. 3). Washington, DC: Gallaudet University.

Johnson, R. E. (1994). Possible influences on bilingualism in early ASL acquisition. *Teaching English to Deaf and Second Language Students, 10*(2), 9–17.

Kahn, J. (2012, July 29). Amazing facts about your senses. *Parade,* 1–3. Retreived from http://www.parade.com/health/2012/07/29-amazing-facts-about-senses.html.

Keller, H. (1957). *The open door.* New York: Doubleday.

Knoors, H., & Marschark, M. (2012). Langauge planning for the 21st century: Revisiting bilingual language policy for deaf children. *Journal of Deaf Studies and Deaf Education, 11,* 291–305. Doi: 10.1093/deafed/enso18.

Komesaroff, L. (2002). *Disabling pedagogy: Power, politics, and Deaf education.* Washington, DC: Gallaudet University Press.

Kuhn, T. S. (1996). *The structure of scientific revolutions.* Chicago: University of Chicago Press.

Ladd, P. (2003). *Understanding deaf culture: In search of deafhood.* Clevedon, UK: Multilingual Matters.

Lane, H. (1984). *When the mind hears: A history of the deaf.* New York: Random House.

Lane, H. (1992). *The mask of benevolence: Disabling the Deaf community.* New York: Knopf.

Lane, H., Hoffmeister, R., & Bahan, B. (1996). *A journey into the Deaf-world.* San Diego, CA: DawnSign Press.

Lane, H., & Grodin, M. (1997). Ethical issues in cochlear implant surgery: An exploration into disease, disability, and the best interests of the child. *Kennedy Institute of Ethics Journal, 7,* 231–251.

Lang, H. (2002). Higher education for deaf students: Research priorities in the new millennium. *Journal of Deaf Studies and Deaf Education, 7,* 267–280.

Lang, H. (2003). Perspectives on the history of deaf education. In M. Marschark & P. E. Spencer (Eds.), *Oxford handbook of deaf studies, language, and education* (pp. 9–20). New York, NY: Oxford University Press.

Lee, D. S., Lee, J. S., Oh, S. H., Kim, S. K., Kim, J. W., Chung, J. K., Lee, M. C., & Kim, C. S. (2001). Cross-modal plasticity and cochlear implants. *Nature. 409,* 149–150.

Leigh, G. R. (2001). Curriculum considerations. In R. G. Beattie (Ed.), *Ethics in deaf education: The first six years* (pp. 143–166). San Diego, CA: Academic Press.

Leigh, I. W., & Pollard, R. Q. (2003). Mental health and deaf adults. In M. Marschark & P. E. Spencer (Eds.), *Oxford handbook of deaf studies, language, and education* (pp. 203–218). New York, NY: Oxford University Press.

Lenneberg, E. (1969). *New directions in the study of language.* Cambridge, MA: MIT Press.

Levitt, H., McGarr, N., & Geffner, D. (1987). Development of language and communication skills in hearing-impaired children: Introduction. *ASHA Monographs, 26,* 1–8.

Lewis, J. J. (2009). About Helen Keller. *About women's history.* Retrieved from http://womenshistory.about.com/od/disabilities/a/qu-helen-keller-2.htm.

Longergan, B. (1957). *Insight: A study of human understanding.* London, UK: Longmans, Green & Co.

Lovat, T. J., & Smith, D. L. (1998). *Curriculum: Action on reflection revisited* (3rd ed.). Katoomba, Australia: Social Science Press.

Luetke-Stahlman, B. (1998). *Language issues in deaf education.* Hillsboro, OR: Butte Publications.

Lynas, W., & Turner, S. (1995). *Young children with sensori-neural hearing loss from ethnic minority families.* Manchester, UK: Centre for Audiology, Education of the Deaf and Speech Pathology, University of Manchester.

Marschark, M. (1993). *Psychological development of deaf children.* New York, NY: Oxford University Press.

Marschark, M., Lang, H. G., & Albertini, J. A. (2002). *Educating deaf students: From research to practice.* New York, NY: Oxford University Press.

Martirano, M. D. (1997, April 23). Students follow the sign. *Cumberland Times-News*, pp. 1–11.

Matthews, T. J., & Reich, C. F. (1993). Constraints on communication in classrooms for the deaf. *American Annals of the Deaf, 138*, 14–18.

Maxwell, M. (1990). Simultaneous communication: The state of the art and proposals for change. Simultaneous communication, American Sign Language, and other classroom modes using signs. *Sign Language Studies, 69*, 333–390.

Mayberry, R. I., & Eichen, E. B. (1991). The long-lasting advantage of learning sign language in childhood: Another look at the critical period for language acquisition. *Journal of Memory and Language, 30*, 486–512.

Mayberry, R. I. (1998). The critical period for language acquisition and the deaf child's language comprehension: A psycholinguistic approach. *Bulletin D'Audiophonologie: Annales Scientifiques De L'Université De Franche-Comté, 15*, 349–358. Retrieved from http://idiom.ucsd.edu/~rmayberry/pubs/ACFOSmayberry.pdf.

Mayberry, R. I., Chen, J-K., Witcher, P., & Klein, D. (2011). Age of acquisition effects on the functional organization of language in the adult brain. *Brain and Language, 119*, 16–29. Retrieved from http://grammar.ucsd.edu/mayberrylab/Publications.html.

McEvoy, C., Marschark, M., & Nelson, D. I. (1999). Comparing the mental lexicons of deaf and hearing individuals. *Journal of Educational Psychology, 91,* 1–9.

Merriam, S. B. (1998). *Qualitative research and case study applications in education.* San Francisco, CA: Jossey-Bass.

Mertens, D. M., Sass-Lehrer, M., & Scott-Olson, K. (2000). Sensitivity in the family-professional relationship: Parental experiences in families with young deaf and hard of hearing children. In P. E. Spencer, C. J. Erting, & M. Marschark (Eds.), *The deaf child in the family and at school* (pp. 133–150). Mahwah, NJ: Lawrence Erlbaum Associates.

Messenheimer-Young, T., & Whitesell, K. (1995). Communication-based learning communities: Coming to know by co-creating curriculum. *Volta Review, 97*(5), iii–vii.

Mindel, E. D., & Vernon, M. (1971). *They grow in silence, the deaf child and his family.* Silver Spring, MD: National Association of the Deaf.

Moeller, M. P., Osberger, M. J., & Eccarius, M. (1986). Language and learning skills of hearing-impaired students: Receptive language skills. *ASHA Monographs, 23,* 41–53.

Moeller, M. P. (2000). Early intervention and language development in children who are deaf and hard of hearing. Sep; 106 (3):E43. Retrieved from http://www.ncbi.nlm.nih.gov/pubmed/10969127.

Moores, D. F. (1996). *Educating the deaf: Psychology, principles, and practices* (4th ed.). Boston, MA: Houghton Mifflin.

Moores, D. F. (2001). *Educating the deaf: Psychology, principles and practices.* Boston, MA: Houghton Mifflin Company.

Myklebust, H. (1957). *Psychology of Deafness.* New York, NY: Grune & Stratton.

Munroe, M. (Producer), & Crider, L. B. & Crider, S. (Writers). (2008). *Summer's story: A collection of videos about life experience with the cochlear implant* [DVD]. Alachua, FL: Munroe MultiMedia.

National Institute of Health (1993, March). Early identification of hearing impairment in infants and young children. *NIH Consensus Statement* 11(1), 1–24. Retrieved from http://consensus.nih.gov/1993/1993hearinginfantschildren092html.htm.

Newport, E., Bavelier, D., & Neville, H. (2001). Critical thinking about critical periods: Perspectives on a critical period for language acquisition. In *Language, Brain, and Cognitive Development Essays in Honor of Jacques Mehler* (pp. 481–502). Cambridge, MA: MIT Press.

Nover, S. (1995). Politics and language: American Sign Language and English in deaf education. In C. Lucas (Ed.), *Sociolinguistics in deaf communities* (pp. 109–163). Washington, DC: Gallaudet University Press.

Nover, S., Christensen, K., & Cheng, L. (1998). Development of ASL and English competence for learners who are deaf. *Topics in Language Disorders, 18,* 61–71.

Ozmon, H. & Craver, S. (2008). *Philosophical foundations of education, Eighth edition.* Upper Saddle River, NJ: Person Prentice Hall.

Padden, C. (1980). The Deaf community and the culture of Deaf people. In C. Baker & R. Battison (Eds.) *Sign language and the Deaf community: Essays in honour of William Stokoe.* Washington DC: National Association of the Deaf.

Padden, C., & Humphries, T. (1988). *Deaf in America: Voices from a culture.* Cambridge, MA: Harvard University Press.

Padden, C., & Humphries, T. (2005). *Inside Deaf culture.* Cambridge, MA: Harvard University Press.

Paludneviciene, R., & Leigh, I. W. (2011). *Cochlear implants: Evolving perspectives.* Washington, DC: Gallaudet University Press.

Patton, M. Q. (2002). *Qualitative research and evaluation methods* (3rd ed.). Thousand Oaks, CA: Sage.

Petitto, L. A. (1993). On manual babbling: New analyses yield new insights into the essence of early language acquisition. *Abstracts of the Society for Research in Child Development. New Orleans, Louisiana,* 540.

Piantanida, M., & Garman, N. (2009). *The qualitative dissertation* (2nd ed.). Thousand Oaks, CA: Sage.

Power, D. (1997). *Constructing lives: The Deaf experience.* Brisbane, Australia: Griffith University, Centre for Deafness Studies and Research.

Power, D., & Leigh, G. R. (2003). Curriculum: Cultural and communicative contexts. In M. Marschark & P. E. Spencer (Eds.), *Oxford handbook of deaf studies, language, and education* (pp. 38–51). New York, NY: Oxford University Press.

Quigley, S. P., & Paul, P. V. (1984). *Language and deafness.* Boston, MA: College-Hill Press.

Ramsey, C. (1989). Language planning in deaf education. In *The sociolinguistics of the Deaf community*, ed. C. Lucas, 123–146. San Diego, CA: Academic Press.

Sacks, O. (1991). *Seeing voices.* London: Picador.

Sacks, O. (1993, May 10). To see and not see. *New Yorker*, 59–73.

Seal, B. C. (1998). *Best practices in educational interpreting.* Boston, MA: Allyn & Bacon.

Schildroth, A. N., & Hotto, S. A. (1996). Changes in student and program characteristics, 1984–85 and 1994–95. *American Annals of the Deaf, 141*, 68–71.

Sharma, A., Dorman, M. F., & Spahr, A. J. (2001). Rapid development of cortical auditory evoked potentials after early cochlear implantation. *NeuroReport, 13*, 1365–1368.

Shepherd, R. K., & Hardie, N. A. (2001). Deafness-induced changes in the auditory pathway: implications for cochlear implants. *Audiology and Neurotology, 6*, 305–318.

Simms, L., & Thumann, H. (2007). In search of a new linguistically and culturally sensitive paradigm in Deaf education. *American Annals of the Deaf, 152*(3), 302–311.

Sparrow, R. (2005). Defending deaf culture: The case of cochlear implants. *Journal of Political Philosophy, 13*(2), 135–152. doi:10.1111/j.1476-9760.2005.00217.x.

Spencer, L. J., Gantz, B. J., & Kuntson, J. F. (2004). Outcomes and achievement of students who grew up with access to cochlear implants. *Laryngoscope, 114,* 1576–1581. Doi:10.1097/00005537-200409000-00014.

Spencer, L., Tomblin, J. B., & Gantz, B. J. (2012). Growing up with a cochlear implant: Education, vocation, and affiliation. *Journal of Deaf Studies and Deaf Education, 17,* 483–498.

Stake, R. E. (1994). Case studies. In N. K. Denzin & Y. S. Lincoln (Eds.), *The handbook of qualitative research* (pp. 236–247). Thousand Oaks, CA: Sage.

Stake, R. E. (1995). *The art of case study.* Thousand Oaks, CA: Sage.

Stewart, D. A., & Kluwin, T. N. (2001). *Teaching deaf and hard of hearing students: Content, strategies and curriculum.* Boston, MA: Allyn & Bacon.

Stokoe, W. C., (1960). *Sign language structure: An outline of the visual communication system of the American Deaf* (Occasional Papers 8). Buffalo, NY: University of Buffalo, Department of Anthropology and Linguistics.

Stokoe, W. (2001). *Language in hand: Why sign came before speech.* Washington, DC: Gallaudet University Press.

Summerfield, A. Q., & Marshall, D. H. (1995). Preoperative predictors of outcomes from cochlear implantation in adults: performance and quality of life. *Annals of Otology, Rhinology, and Laryngology,* Suppl. 166, 105–108.

Supalla, S. (1991). Manually coded English: The modality question in signed language development. In P. Siple & S. Fischer (Eds.), *Theoretical issues in sign language research* (Vol. 2). Chicago, IL: University of Chicago Press.

Svartholm, K. (1993). Bilingual education for the deaf in Sweden. *Sign Language Studies, 81,* 291–332.

Svartholm, K. (1994). Second language learning in the deaf. In I. Ahlgren & K. Hyltenstam (Eds.), *Bilingualism in deaf education* (pp. 61–70). Hamburg, Germany: Signum.

Svirsky, M. A., Robbin, A. M., Kirk, K. I., Pisoni, D. B., & Miyamoto, R. T. (2000). Language development in profoundly deaf children with cochlear implants. *American Psychological Society, 11*(2), 153–158.

Taylor, G., & Bishop, J. (Eds.). (1991). *Being deaf: The experience of deafness.* London, UK: Pinter & The Open University.

Tomblin, B. J., Barker, B. A., Spencer, L. J., Zhang, X., & Gantz, B. J. (2005). The effect of age at cochlear implant initial stimulation on expressive language growth infants and toddlers. *Journal of Speech, Language and Hearing Research, 48,* 853–867.

Traxler, C. B. (2000). Measuring up to performance standards in reading and mathematics: Achievement of selected deaf and hard of hearing students in the national norming of the 9th Edition Stanford Achievement Test. *Journal of Deaf Studies and Deaf Education, 5,* 337–348.

Van Cleve, J. V., & Crouch, B. A. (1989). *A place of their own: Creating the Deaf community in America.* Washington, DC: Gallaudet University Press.

Verbist, A. (2010). *The acquisition of personal pronouns in cochlear implanted children.* (Dissertation). Leiden University. LOT Dissertational Series 242. Retrieved from http://www.lotpublications.nl.

Watson, L., & Parsons, J. (1998). Supporting deaf pupils in mainstream settings. In S. Gregory, P. Knight, W. McCracken, S. Power, & L. Watson (Eds.), *Issues in deaf education* (pp. 135–142). London: Fulton.

Weinberg, N., & Sterritt, M. (1986). Disability and identity: A study of identity patterns in adolescents with hearing impairments. *Rehabilitation Psychology, 31*(2), 95–102.

Wilson, B. S., & Dorman, M. F. (2008). Cochlear implants: a remarkable past and a brilliant future. Retrieved from: http://www.ncbi.nlm.nih.gov/pmc/articles/PMC3707130/.

Wittgenstein, L. (1922). Tractus logico-philosophicus. In C. K. Ogden, (Ed.), *International Library of Psychology and Scientific Method* (pp. 7–189). New York, NY: Harcourt, Brace.

Woll, B., & Ladd, P. (2003). Deaf communities. In M. Marschark & P. E. Spencer (Eds.), *Oxford handbook of deaf studies, language, and education* (pp. 151–163). New York: Oxford University Press.

Wood, D., Wood, H., Griffiths, A., & Howarth, I. (1986). *Teaching and talking with deaf children*. Chichester, UK: Wiley.

Woodward, J. (1982). *How you gonna get to heaven, if you can't talk to Jesus: On Depathologizing deafness*. Silver Spring, MD: TJ Publishers.

Yin, R. K. (2003). *Case study research design and methods*. Thousand Oaks, CA: Sage Publications.

Yoshinaga-Itano, C. (2003). From screening to early identification and intervention: Discovering predictors to successful outcomes for children with significant hearing loss. *Journal of Deaf Studies and Deaf Education* 8(1), 11–30. Retrieved on February 20, 2013, from http://jdsde.oxfordjournals.org/content/8/1/11.full.pdf+html.

Index

Illustrations and photographs are indicated by page numbers in italics.

ABR (auditory brain-stem response) evaluations, 61, 70
"Advances in the Genetics of Deafness" (Arnos & Pandya), 32
Agricola, Rudolf, 16
American School for the Deaf, 19
American Sign Language (ASL)
  acceptance of, 32
  bilingual-bicultural approach, 6, 24, 32–33, 75, 123
  cochlear implants, use with, 23–24, 44, 82–83
  critical period for acquisition of, 48
  Daniels family's use of, 2, 6–7, 66–68, 68, 75, 83
  as full-fledged language, 6, 22, 24
  hearing aids, use with, 24
  language acquisition enhanced by, 23–24
  oralist views of, 20
  as visual-spatial language, 24
amplification systems, 52–55, 70–71. *See also* cochlear implants (CIs); hearing aids
Aristotle, 14
Arnos, K., 32
ASL. *See* American Sign Language
auditory brain-stem response (ABR) evaluations, 61, 70
auditory movement, 23

auditory training, 23, 54, 70
Australia, Deaf community in, 29

Bahan, B., 32
banking concept of education, 27
Behar, Ruth, 129
behind-the-ear hearing aids, 54, 70
Bell, Alexander Graham, 19
bias in philosophical approaches to Deaf education, 123
bilingual-bicultural (BiBi) approach, 6, 24, 32–33, 75, 123
biologically constrained learning, 47
Bonet, Juan Pablo, 16
border crossings, 129–32
brain hemispheres and creative abilities, 90
bridge-building tools, 4
Buber, Martin, 125, 126, 127
Bulwer, John, 16

Cardano, Girolamo, 16
Children of a Lesser God (Medoff), 26–27
Chirologia (Bulwer), 16
Chorost, Michael, 42, 136
Civil Rights movement, 28
Clerc, Laurent, 18–19

cochlear implants (CIs)
  age of implant, FDA regulations
    on, 54
  ASL, use with, 23–24, 44, 82–83
  criteria for receiving, 75–76
  criticisms of, 80, 118–19, 134–35
  hearing aids vs., 7–8, 79
  Kyler's use of, 10, 75–79, 78–79,
    82–85, 102, 111–14, 117
  mapping process for, 84–85, 112–13
  oralist advocacy of, 23
  quality of life assessments for re-
    cipients of, 119–22
  technological advances in, 112
  time considerations for, 78, 80–82
Cochlear Implants: Evolving Perspec-
  tives (Paludneviciene &
  Leigh), 136
cocooned educational environment,
  benefits of, 127–29
Cogswell, Mason Fitch, 18
collaboration
  in bilingual-bicultural model of
    education, 6, 24, 32–33, 75, 123
  between professionals and fami-
    lies, 133
  between public and residential
    schools, 8, 88–89, 92, 93
college experiences, 10, 108–11
communication, function of, 50
Connecticut Asylum for the Education and Instruction of Deaf
  and Dumb Persons, 19
Cratylus (Plato), 14
creative abilities, brain hemispheres
  and, 90
critical period of language acquisition, 47–50

curriculum
  deafness perspectives influenc-
    ing design of, 34–35
  defined, 33
  hidden curriculum, 33–34
  language acquisition objectives
    and, 35–37

Dalgarno, George, 16–17
Daniels, family overview, 1, 5–6
Daniels, Bob (father)
  ASL use of, 6
  background of, 5–6, 59
  border crossings, 131
  on cochlear implants, 76–77
  reaction to Kyler's deafness, 1,
    62–63
Daniels, Ginny (mother)
  acceptance of Kyler's deafness,
    85–86, 87
  anticipation of Kyler's birth,
    58–60
  ASL use of, 6, 7, 75
  background of, 5–6, 59
  border crossings, 131
  career as teacher and caregiver
    as preparation for raising
    Deaf child, 85–86, 127
  on cochlear implants, 76, 77–79,
    80, 82–83, 85
  deafness as perceived by, 116
  faith, role in life of, 86–87, 126–27
  initial interaction with Getty,
    65–68
  as interpreter for Kyler, 105
  on peer relationships, 93
  reaction to Kyler's deafness, 62, 63
  on school choice, 92, 93

school events, participation in, 94
vocabulary diary of, 67–68, 69
Daniels, Kyler
   artistic abilities of, 89–90, 90, 97,
      98, 102, 106, 106–7, 111
   ASL use of, 2, 6–7, 66–68, 68, 75, 83
   birth of, 59
   border crossings, 130–31
   career aspirations, 111, 120
   cochlear implants of, 10, 75–79,
      78–79, 82–85, 102, 111–14, 117
   cocooned educational environ-
      ment, benefits of, 127–29
   college experiences, 10, 108–11
   communication challenges, 114–
      15, 116
   community involvement, 105–6
   deafness as perceived by,
      116 –17, 127
   demographics and family back-
      ground, 5–6
   detection of hearing loss, 1, 5,
      61–63
   early intervention services re-
      ceived by, 71–72
   elementary school experiences,
      7–8, 88–89, 91–94, 95
   extracurricular activities, 10,
      101, 105
   faith, role in life of, 87, 127
   family support received by,
      72, 134
   hearing aids fitted for, 6, 70–71
   high school experiences, 9–10,
      102–6
   individualized education program
      (IEP), 91, 94–95
   initial interaction with Getty, 65–68
   middle school experiences, 8–9,
      94–102
   peer relationships, 9–10, 93–94,
      98, 106, 110–11, 113–14
   pets, importance to, 99–101, 101
   preschool years, 60–61, 60, 68–69
   on school choice, 92
   self-assessment of quality of life,
      119–21, 122
   speech therapy received by, 7, 9,
      92, 95, 104
Dark Ages, attitudes toward Deaf
   in, 14–15
Deaf and Dumbe Man's Friend (Bulwer), 16
"The Deaf and Dumb in Antiquity"
   (*New York Times*), 14–15
Deaf community
   in Australia, 29
   challenges facing, 31
   disability construction of, 32
   diversity within, 114
   establishment of, 19
   language-minority construction
      of, 32
   oppression of, 29–32
Deaf education. *See also* curriculum
   barriers to, 30, 39–40, 122, 123
   bias in philosophical approaches
      to, 123
   bilingual-bicultural approach to,
      6, 24, 32–33, 75, 123
   border crossings needed in,
      131–32
   boundaries imposed by philoso-
      phies of, 3, 123
   cocooned environment, benefits
      of, 127–29

Deaf education *(Continued)*
  future research needs, 37–39
  history of, 15–21
  legislation impacting, 31, 102
  literacy levels, 73–74
  manualist approach to, 17, 18
  oralist approach to, 18, 19–20,
    22–23, 24
  parents, decisions facing, 13, 25,
    37, 43–46
  policy and planning, need for re-
    examination of, 135–38
  prescriptive approach to, 40
  Total Communication philoso-
    phy of, 7, 73, 74–75
Deaf Identity Scale, 119, 120–21
Deafness
  annual births resulting in, 41
  dilemmas of, 43–46
  early detection and stimulation,
    importance of, 46–52
  family support, importance of,
    51–52, 72, 134
  genetic deafness, 31–32
  historical views on, 14–16, 22
  language acquisition, impact on,
    50–52
  parental reactions to, 41–43
  perceptions of, 116–17, 127
Deaf President Now movement
  (1988), 28–29, 122–23
Descartes, René, 17
Diamant, Anita, 128
Diener, E., 120
Digby, Kenelm, 16
digital hearing aids, 24, 53
disability construction of Deaf community, 32

*Disabling Pedagogy: Power, Politics,
  and Deaf Education* (Komesaroff), 29
diversity within Deaf community, 114
Drawing on the Right Side of the Brain
  (Edwards), 89–90
Dual Identity scale, 121

early detection and stimulation, importance of, 46–52
Early Hearing Detection and Intervention (EHDI) programs, 51
The Educational Imagination (Eisner),
  138
educational interpreters. *See* interpreters
Education for All Handicapped
  Children Act of 1975, 31
Edwards, Betty, 89–90
Eisner, Elliot, 90, 138
elementary school experiences, 7–8,
  88–89, 91–94, 95
English/ASL bilingualism, 6, 24,
  32–33, 75, 123
extracurricular activities, 10, 101, 105

faith, role in life of Daniels family,
  86–87, 126–27
family support, importance of, 51–
  52, 72, 134
Ferris, Caren, 45
FM systems, 53, 70
Food and Drug Administration
  (FDA), 54
Freire, Paulo, 27–28, 29, 30

Gallaudet, Thomas Hopkins, 18–19
Gallaudet University, 28–29, 45–46,
  122–23

Garretson, Merv, 132
Geizen, M. R., 23–24
genetic deafness, 31–32
gesture, in language acquisition process, 14
Getty, Ann Darby
  border crossings with Daniels family, 130
  as educational interpreter, 8–9, 86, 92
  initial interaction with Daniels family, 65–68
  involvement with Deaf community, 1, 63–64, 86, 104
  motivations for writing book, 3–4, 135
  relationship with Kyler outside of school, 96
  research methods of, 1, 2
  role in Kyler's education, 8–9, 92, 104
  satellite program initiated by, 88–89
  on title of project, 4, 132–33
Grosjean, F., 33
"Growing Up with a Cochlear Implant: Education, Vocation, and Affiliation" (Spencer et al.), 119

Hammerstein, Oscar, II, 4
hearing aids
  age for fitting children with, 54
  ASL, use with, 24
  behind-the-ear, 54, 70
  cochlear implants vs., 7–8, 79
  digital, 24, 53
  Kyler fitted with, 6, 70–71
  oralist advocacy of, 23

hearing identity subscale, 120, 121
hearing screening, 5, 51, 61–62
Heinicke, Samuel, 18
hidden curriculum, 33–34
high school experiences, 9–10, 102–6
Hoffmeister, R., 32
hope for positive outcome, importance of maintaining, 55, 57, 124–25
houseparents, 21
Human Genome Project, 31
Humphries, T., 32

I and Thou (Buber), 125
"I-It" relationships, 125–26
inclusion environments, 7, 8
individualized education programs (IEPs), 91, 94–95
Institution Nationale des Sourds-Muets á Paris, 17
interpreters, 9, 36, 104–5, 108–9, 110
"I-Thou" relationships, 125, 126

Jordan, I. King, 29

Kahn, Jennifer, 47
Keller, Helen, 29–30, 55
Kingsley, Emily Pearl, 56–57
Kinniburgh, Robert, 18
Kluwin, T. N., 35
Knoors, Harry, 24, 135–36, 137
Komesaroff, Linda, 29, 30

Ladd, P., 14
Lane, Harlan, 15–16, 26, 32, 38
Lang, Harry, 37

language
  function of, 29, 50
  policy and planning, need for re-
    examination of, 135–38
  speech vs., 30
language acquisition
  ASL enhancing, 23–24
  critical period of, 47–50
  curriculum influenced by, 35–37
  deafness, impact on, 50–52
  evolutionary speculation on, 14
  sensitive period of, 47, 49
Language and Deafness (Quigley &
  Paul), 73
language-minority construction of
  Deaf community, 32
"Language Planning for the 21st Century: Revisiting Bilingual Language Policy for Deaf Children" (Knoors & Marschark),
  135–36
least restrictive environments, 31
Leigh, G. R., 35
Leigh, I. W., 34–35, 136
Lenneberg, Eric, 47
L'Epée, Charles Michel de, 17, 18
liberation from oppression, 27–28
lipreading, 17, 23
listening skills, 54
literacy levels, 73–74
Lonergan, Bernard, 123

magnetic resonance imaging
  (MRI), 47
manualism, 17, 18
mapping process for cochlear implants, 84–85, 112–13
Marschark, Marc, 24, 135–36, 137

*The Mask of Benevolence: Disabling the
  Deaf Community* (Lane), 26
Massieu, Jean, 18–19
Mayberry, Rachel, 48
Medoff, Mark, 26
Merriam, Sharon, 135
methodical signs, 17
middle school experiences, 8–9,
  94–102
Moeller, M. P., 51–52
MRI (magnetic resonance imaging), 47
Multicultural Art Contest, 97, 98
multisensory learning, 16

National Center for Hearing Assessment and Management, 51
National Institutes of Health (NIH),
  31, 50–51
Naturall Language of the Hand (Bulwer), 16
natural sign language, 17, 19
neonatal hearing screening, 5, 51,
  61–62
No Child Left Behind Act of 2001
  (NCLB), 9, 103
normalcy, oralist views of, 23
Nucleus 22-Channel Cochlear Implant System, 79

oppression
  of Deaf community, 29–32
  defined, 27
  liberation from, 27–28
  oralism, 18, 19–20, 22–23, 24

Padden, C., 32
Paludneviciene, R., 136

Pandya, A., 32
parents
    education decisions facing, 13, 25, 43–46
    hope for positive outcome, importance of maintaining, 55, 57, 124–25
    involvement in Deaf education, 37
    reactions to child's deafness, 41–43
Paul, Peter, 73
peer relationships, 9–10, 93–94, 98, 106, 110–11, 113–14
Pereire, Jacobo, 17
Philocopus (Bulwer), 16
Phonic Ear FM systems, 70
Ponce de León, Pedro, 15–16
positron emission tomography (PET), 47
Power, D., 35
preschool years, 60, 60–61, 68–69
prescriptive educational approach, 40
Public Law 94-142, 31
public schools
    collaboration with residential schools, 8, 88–89, 92, 93
    self-contained classrooms, 7, 8, 9, 91, 94

quality of life assessments, 119–22
Quigley, Stephen, 73

Rebuilt: My Journey Back to the Hearing World (Chorost), 136
The Red Tent (Diamant), 128
The Reduction of Letters and the Art of Teaching the Mute to Speak (Bonet), 16

Registry of Interpreters for the Deaf, 104
residential schools
    characteristics of, 21
    collaboration with public schools, 8, 88–89, 92, 93
    decline of, 30–31
    establishment of, 19
    satellite program, 88–89
    teaching methods of, 20–21
residual hearing, 6, 18, 70, 74
Rousseau, Jean-Jacques, 17
Royce, Josiah, 50

Satisfaction with Life Scale (SWLS), 119–20
school experiences. *See also* public schools; residential schools
    college, 10, 108–11
    elementary school, 7–8, 88–89, 91–94, 95
    high school, 9–10, 102–6
    middle school, 8–9, 94 102
screening for hearing loss, 5, 51, 61–62
self-contained classrooms, 7, 8, 9, 91, 94
semiotic theory, 17
sensitive period of language acquisition, 47, 49
Sicard, Roch-Ambroise Cucurron, 18–19
Signed English, 7
Socrates, 14
Sparrow, R., 118–19
speech vs. language, 30
speech coding and recoding, 73, 74
speechreading, 17, 23
speech therapy, 7, 9, 23, 92, 95, 104
Spencer, L., 119, 120, 121–22

Steinberg, David, 48–49
Sterritt, M., 120, 121–22
Stewart, D. A., 35
Stokoe, William, 22
SWLS (Satisfaction with Life Scale),
     119–20

Talmud, 14
Tarra, Giulio, 19–20
Tomblin, J. B., 119
Total Communication philosophy, 7,
     73, 74–75
Translated Woman (Behar), 129

Vernon, McCay, 42, 43
vibrotactile aids, 6, 70
vocabulary diary, 67–68, 69

Weinberg, N., 120, 121–22
"Welcome to Holland" (Kingsley),
     56–57
Wittgenstein, Ludwig, 50
Woodward, James, 10, 115–16

Yoshinaga-Itano, C., 52

Zinser, Elisabeth, 29